Carl Becker's Heavenly City Revisited

Studies Resulting from a Symposium Held at
Colgate University, Hamilton, New York
October 13, 1956
as a Phase of the Sixth Annual Meeting of the
New York State Association of European Historians

Carl Becker's
Heavenly City Revisited

Edited by

RAYMOND O. ROCKWOOD

Cornell University Press

ITHACA, NEW YORK

This work has been brought to publication with the assistance of a grant from the Ford Foundation.

CORNELL   UNIVERSITY   PRESS

First published 1958

PRINTED IN THE UNITED STATES OF AMERICA BY THE

VAIL-BALLOU PRESS, INC., BINGHAMTON, NEW YORK

Preface

THROUGHOUT his scholarly career, Carl Lotus Becker contemplated great issues confronting both professional historians and contemporary Americans. His humane personality and sensitive, quizzical mind, ever in search of the meaning of human events, have left an indelible impression upon this generation. He erected a formidable and unforgettable monument to his own memory through the urbane wit, polished charm, and shrewd penetration of his many writings. He attracted all men who welcome an invitation to significant thinking. The caliber and productive scholarship of his distinguished students are impressive tribute to his intellectual influence. He challenged his fellow craftsmen to take stock of their method, brought the philosophy and science of his day to focus upon his investigations, scrutinized and reassessed the origins of his own democratic tradition, and, above all, wrestled constantly with the meaning of freedom in its twentieth-century context. The impact of his personality and character is revealed in the profound devotion of his students.

His most popular and, if the present volume is any indication, his most controversial work was *The Heavenly City of the Eighteenth-Century Philosophers.*[1] First pub-

[1] New Haven: Yale University Press, 1932.

lished in 1932 (as a result of a series of lectures delivered at Yale University the year before), the work has now passed into its tenth printing, and, if sales figures are any criterion, its popularity is certainly not on the wane.[2] During the first decade after its publication, some 2,500 copies were sold, another 5,500 were purchased during the next ten years, and since 1951 the sales have passed the 3,200 mark.

The present volume is the unpremeditated dividend of an all-day symposium on *The Heavenly City* held at Colgate University, Hamilton, New York, October 13, 1956, as a phase of the Sixth Annual Meeting of the New York State Association of European Historians. Primarily a record of the somewhat informal proceedings, these studies are also an invitation to an appreciation and re-assessment of Becker's book. While the evaluation of a single work calls for an understanding of its place in the total context of the author's life and thought and may, in turn, throw light upon them both, it cannot presume to do more than weigh one aspect of a multidimensional and significant career. For this exercise in intellectual history Becker himself has provided the yardstick. It requires "precise knowledge" and "imaginative understanding." The surest road to failure, he wisely noted, is for one to "cultivate a capacity for being irritated by the ignorance and foolishness of his predecessors."[3]

Ever since its publication, *The Heavenly City* has been acclaimed by the public and profession as a whole for its

[2] Letter dated March 8, 1957, from Chester Kerr, secretary, Yale University Press, to the author.

[3] "What Is Historiography?" *American Historical Review*, XLIV (Oct., 1938), 22.

literary merit and its novel and provocative interpretation.

An appreciative reader will not wish that even a single chapter had been added to *The Heavenly City*. The very perfection with which he did the thing he did was itself a limitation. No one knew this better than Becker, and he accepted the limitation freely as the price to be paid for what he chose to do.[4]

Treating the eighteenth century as a way station between the medieval and modern climates of opinion, Becker turned Humpty Dumpty upside down by emphasizing the discontinuity between the Enlightenment and the twentieth century and by speculating on the affinity of the Age of Voltaire with that of Aquinas.

The reception of the volume at the time of publication, though generally enthusiastic, was not entirely uncritical, and, despite its appealing qualities, many scholars have no doubt generally utilized *The Heavenly City* with due circumspection and recognition of its legitimate scope and possible limitations.

In 1932, for instance, Max Lerner, a close friend of Becker, wrote a five-page commentary on *The Heavenly City* for the *Yale Law Review*.[5] "Here is a book," he wrote, "so simple, so light, so clear that one feels didactic in pointing out that it is really a scholarly study in the history of ideas, and a bit ponderous in assessing it (as it

---

[4] George H. Sabine, "Carl Lotus Becker," in Carl Becker, *Freedom and Responsibility in the American Way of Life* (New York, 1946), p. xiv.

[5] XLII (May, 1933), 1143–1148; reprinted in Lerner's *Ideas Are Weapons* (New York, 1933), 235–243.

must none the less be assessed) a classic." The general tone of the review reflects profound respect for a distinguished American scholar. And yet Mr. Lerner raises some fundamental doubts. "This picture of the eighteenth-century mind drawn for us in vivid strokes by the author is, some will fear, perhaps too brilliant to be fair and too pat to be sound." Praising Becker for his success in capturing "the mind and mood of a whole age," Mr. Lerner suggests that the analysis would be more convincing "if he had introduced into it some of the roughnesses and loose ends that we see around us in our own age, and had been less insistent on making out of it a paradox within a unity." Becker tries to pour into the same mold the thinking of people who span several generations and who face "widely variant situations." Moreover, as intellectuals, they represented only themselves and the middle classes. More serious, Becker "leaves out of account the whole play of economic and political forces out of which ideas grow. He is so concerned with giving us the climate of opinion that he forgets about the soil of opinion."

Other scholars introduced various question marks. Ira O. Wade ̄of Princeton qualified his judgment in a review published in the *Journal of Modern History* in 1933:

The [lectures] are graceful and witty, and present an original, if not altogether convincing, view of the intellectual movement in the eighteenth century. . . . With Mr. Becker's interpretations, however, one may be permitted to disagree. . . . It is not at all certain that the "new history" grew out of the problem of good and evil. Nevertheless, one may disregard Mr. Becker's general thesis, his logical arrangements, and his

Preface

explanations, and still find in his essays stimulating points which make his book worthy of a careful reading.[6]

More severe was Marjorie S. Harris of Randolph-Macon Woman's College, who, after referring to the "four brilliant and erudite lectures" and outlining the general argument of the book, devoted over two pages of her review in the *Journal of Philosophy* to an extended series of doubts. Her conclusions were, in brief:

Though Mr. Becker questions the modernity of aspects of eighteenth-century thought because he finds evidence of overrationalization, the chief defect of his book is just this tendency. . . . In spite of its many excellencies, the book demonstrates the fact that in one modern scholar the love of abstract speculation still persists.[7]

Even more critical than any of these were the strictures of Ronald S. Crane in a course on eighteenth-century thought the present writer attended at the University of Chicago in 1933–1934, views more recently recorded in Volume I of *English Literature, 1660–1800: A Bibliography of Modern Studies* published in 1950.[8]

[6] V (June, 1933), 233–235.
[7] XXX (March, 1933), 191–193.
[8] I (Princeton, 1950), 104–106.
"From Becker's thesis as thus stated [namely, that the *philosophes* remade the City of St. Augustine into their own Heavenly City] it is not likely that any one will seriously dissent; the difficulty is with his treatment of details. And here he is handicapped to begin with by inadequate command of the general intellectual tradition inherited from antiquity and the middle ages. . . .
"Unfortunately he is equally reckless in dealing with some of the writers whom his special purpose in his lectures should have

Preface

How many casual readers have been aware of such reservations is a question. The rather general tendency of students to turn to the volume for a comprehensive, definitive, and self-sufficient synthesis of the Enlightenment warrants the reconsideration of the work in the symposium represented by this volume. Close inspection may or may not reveal doubts, but the finesse of Becker's argument still leaves open the problem of a full appreciation of the work for what it was and was not.

If Becker chose, for purposes of argument, to look at the Enlightenment as though it were more closely akin to the medieval than the modern mind, he certainly reminded the reader by the very use in his title of the phrase "climate of opinion" that he was aware that, whatever the abstract identities and ideological interrelations, these two were distinct movements to be understood ultimately in the context of each age. One might ask the question, As a modern mind endeavoring to compare these three climates, was Becker himself inspecting all

---

induced him to read with more than ordinary care. Galileo and Locke are instances in point. . . .

"This occasional distortion of the meaning of individual writers is less distressing, however, than the obscurity and confusion in which Becker frequently involves his exposition when he is characterizing movements of thought. These traits are especially evident in his second and third lectures . . . and thus are attributable, in great part, to a failure to recognize how dangerously multivocal were many of the crucial terms in which the 'philosophers' were accustomed to express their ideas. To take over into one's own writing such systematically ambiguous words as 'reason,' or 'nature,' . . . without first having explored analytically the whole range of their possible and actual connotations, is to court inevitable disaster when one attempts to deal with conflicts or transitions of thought in which their meanings are involved."

three from the vantage point of modern materialism to which he was personally committed? The suggestion that Becker was evidently detaching himself from all three climates is not necessarily to dissociate him from his own pragmatic orientation. Certainly, in the light of his presidential address, "Everyman His Own Historian," and of everything he had said earlier about the flimsy substructure of historical "facts," his reference to "hard facts," "brute facts," and "irreducible facts" to describe the modern mind would suggest such detachment.

The design of *The Heavenly City* is best illuminated when it is viewed as an integral part of the pattern of Becker's larger concerns. Relevant threads can be traced to his earliest writing. The message of *The Heavenly City* is also sharpened when read in the light of other works written by him about the same time: *Modern History*, "Everyman His Own Historian," and "Liberalism— A Way Station." [9] Such perspective on Becker's thought can be found in excellent studies already published [10] and in papers included in this volume. It is not inappropriate to take note briefly here, as a basis for better understanding of *The Heavenly City*, of his earlier reflec-

[9] *Modern History: The Rise of a Democratic, Scientific and Industrialized Civilization* (New York, 1931); the two essays were reprinted in *Everyman His Own Historian* (New York, 1935), 91–100 and 233–255.

[10] Leo Gershoy, "Carl Becker on Progress and Power," *American Historical Review*, LX (Oct., 1949), 22–35; Louis Gottschalk, "Carl Becker: Skeptic or Humanist?" *Journal of Modern History*, XVII (June, 1946), 160–162; Sabine, *op. cit.*; Charlotte Watkins Smith, *Carl Becker: On History and the Climate of Opinion* (Ithaca, N.Y., 1956); David W. Noble, "Carl Becker: Science, Relativism, and the Dilemma of Diderot," *Ethics*, LXVII (July, 1957), 233–248.

Preface

tions on the interrelation of eighteenth-century ideas and institutions and of his comments on the novelty of these ideas and their relation to medieval thought.

What conception of the role of rationalism in the dynamics of eighteenth-century life in France and America emerges from his earlier writing? As Professor Gottschalk has noted, the early Becker, a product of Frederick Jackson Turner, sought to rectify the exaggerated tendency of the Turner school to concentrate on the purely American origins of the American tradition by reasserting the importance of its European roots.[11] Long before 1776, Becker affirms many times, Enlightenment ideas were unconsciously upheld and ultimately they represented the "common sense" of their situation to colonial Americans.

Locke did not need to convince the colonists because they were already convinced; and they were already convinced because they had long been living under governments which did, in a rough and ready way, conform to the kind of government for which Locke furnished a reasoned foundation. . . . The general philosophy which lifted this common sense conclusion to the level of a cosmic law, the colonists therefore accepted, during the course of the eighteenth century, without difficulty, almost unconsciously.[12]

In his various books on the background of the American Revolution, Becker recognizes the philosophy of the Enlightenment as a rationalization that is meaningful because it reflects and is organically related to the institutional life of the colonies. If one is in doubt about Becker's

[11] Gottschalk, *op. cit.,* 160.
[12] *The Declaration of Independence: A Study in the History of Political Ideas* (New York, 1922), 72–73.

position, he need only read his delightful, imaginary story of Jeremiah Wynkoop's conversion to the revolutionary cause in *The Spirit of 1776*.[13] And if eighteenth-century rationalism was the unconscious "common sense" of a living situation before 1776 and the explicit rationalization of a program of action resulting in independence, Becker still discovered the real root of American democracy not in ideas borrowed from the Old World, but in the basic economic equality fostered by the bountiful and expansive new environment. In his *Our Great Experiment in Democracy*, itself an essay on novelty and change, first published in 1920, Becker observes:

The story of this steady advance across the continent is the great epic of American history—a New World crusade for the conquest of the wilderness. . . . But there is more in this story than the tale of adventure; rightly told, it will reveal the secret of American history—the persistence of democratic ideals which flourish in the simple and primitive conditions of a frontier society. The influence upon the United States of this century of expansion westward, involving in every generation a return to simple and primitive conditions of life, can be more easily understood if we try to imagine what would have happened if the Pacific had in fact, as the first settlers imagined, washed the western slopes of the Alleghanies. In that case, the United States, confined to the Atlantic coast regions, would no doubt have rapidly come to be a thickly populated country, with little free land, with a consequent rapid development of industrial and social conditions similar to those in European countries. Economic dependence upon Europe would have involved close political relations, and close political relations would have implied a similar if

[13] *The Spirit of 1776 and Other Essays* (Washington, 1927).

not an imitated culture. The United States never could have turned its back on the Old World, and its ideas and its ideals would have been borrowed from London and Paris.[14]

Moreover, in his treatment of the antecedents of the French Revolution in his *Modern History,* published in 1931 while he was writing *The Heavenly City,* Becker presents the *philosophe* movement as a novel response to an eighteenth-century condition. Again and again he refers to the ideas of the liberal thinkers, not as eighteenth-century borrowings from medieval scholasticism, but as *new ideas.* Before the French Revolution took place, he notes, it had already been accomplished in the minds of Frenchmen:

This revolution in men's minds—in their way of thinking— came about very slowly, and perhaps we should call it an evolution rather than a revolution. But at least we may say that by the eighteenth century most educated people had come to have new ideas about the material world and about the world of human society.[15]

New ideas about things and their relations, he states, were developing in early modern times under the impact of a new force, science.

When did people cease to fear the secret forces of nature? When did they cease to think of them as evil forces to be shunned, and come to think of them as beneficent forces to be mastered and made use of? The silent change which took place in people's ideas about nature and her laws is one of the most important events in modern history.[16]

He goes out of his way to contrast the new ideas with the older views upheld in the Middle Ages:

[14] (New York, 1927), 160–161. [15] Page 175. [16] *Ibid.,* 176.

Preface

What was this new idea of the world and of man's place in it? We can best understand what it was by contrasting it with the older idea which had survived from the Middle Ages. . . . This new idea that God had given men reason and intended them to use it was a terrible explosive. If it got into the heads of ordinary people it was sure to upset kings and destroy the power of bishops and popes.[17]

Becker is not doctrinaire in his views of the relationship of ideas and institutions. On the contrary, he sees them as functionally interrelated. One senses that although, in America, ideas do play a creative role, they were not as decisive and explosive a force in that revolutionary situation as they were in France. In America ideas emerge as the natural concomitant of a fortunate circumstance. In France they appear as the negative reaction to an evil condition and an ideal expression of social order yet to be achieved. One concludes that, when Becker bemused himself with an effort to equate the eighteenth-century mind with that of the Middle Ages in *The Heavenly City,* he was doing so in full awareness that the two epochs were essentially different ideologically, each to be comprehended in its own historic context. Ever fascinated with the more abstract aspects of history,[18] Becker embarked upon the writing of his lectures—"this scholastic discussion," he describes his enterprise at one point [19]—to pursue a subject that had long since interested him, namely, the identities of two movements of thought normally, and for reasons of which he was aware, considered dissimilar. In his *The Declaration of Independence,* he underlines these continuities:

[17] *Ibid.,* 187–188.   [18] Sabine, *op. cit.,* p. xiii.
[19] *Heavenly City,* 121.

Preface

The concept of Nature which held the field in the eighteenth century seems at first sight very different from this [of Aquinas]; but the difference is after all mainly on the surface. The eighteenth century did not abandon the old effort to share in the mind of God; it only went about it with greater confidence, and had at last the presumption to think that the infinite mind of God and finite mind of man were one and the same thing.[20]

Or again:

Thus the eighteenth century, having apparently ventured so far afield, is nevertheless to be found within hailing distance of the thirteenth; for its conception of natural law in the world of human relations was essentially identical, as Thomas Aquinas' conception had been, with right reason. It is true that right reason had a much freer field in the eighteenth century than in the thirteenth; it was not limited either by special revelation or by an established Church.[21]

Whether his effort to elaborate on this particular and intriguing hypothesis regarding the abstract content of eighteenth-century thought in *The Heavenly City* has contributed new insight or has tended to distort the true meaning of the Enlightenment is one of the central issues analyzed by members of the symposium.

Certainly Becker chose a theme that was appropriate to the moment. He was speaking to an audience of young men soon to emerge into the harsh realities of a world caught in the floodtide of a depression. Would not a message that called attention to the great gulf between contemporary actuality and the eighteenth-century promise of liberalism arouse a sympathetic response? And would not an analysis which, in a kindly, somewhat jesting

[20] Page 39.   [21] *Ibid.*, 61.

fashion, equated the abstractions of eighteenth-century reason with medieval scholasticism produce that same nod of knowing approval that the *philosophes* were once wont to draw from their readers? Might not a mind like Becker's oriented toward the pragmatic viewpoint be more apt than another to belittle the differences between the ideologies of the two periods as equally absolutist and doctrinaire? Thus his references to the naïveté of the *philosophes* and his frequent comments on the history of liberalism and the dilemma of the liberal in the twentieth century suggest at least one personal vantage point from which Becker was writing *The Heavenly City*. And is this genuine concern for the history and destiny of freedom essentially, from another perspective, a reflection of a long-standing basic ethical concern? As Mr. Gottschalk suggests, this concern may be another fruitful approach to an understanding of *The Heavenly City*.[22]

As an integral expression of Becker's total thought, *The Heavenly City of the Eighteenth-Century Philosophers* must be comprehended in its relation to his earlier writing, to his personal concern for the problem of freedom in its contemporary context, and to other works he was writing at approximately the same time. Inextricably involved in any understanding of the book are his earlier reflections on the role of the Philosophers in the two revolutionary situations, the course of liberalism, the nature of the historical method, and, above all, the dilemma of American democracy in the face of industrialism, new scientific theories, World War, and depression. Perhaps Becker was inadvertently providing us with a key to his own book when he suggested that *Mont-St.-Michel and*

[22] *Infra,* 89ff.

Chartres "throws a highly diffused, stained glass light on the mind of Henry Adams." [23]

Facts do not speak for themselves, said Becker. They inevitably reflect the climate of opinion of the writer, who necessarily writes for Mr. Everyman. Above all, history is disciplined reflection upon the past. Here, in *The Heavenly City*, are some reflections, suggestive, significantly relevant to the problem of Mr. Everyman, tentative as most historical insight must be, suggestively hypothetical, hopefully provocative, and—given the self-imposed limits—necessarily partial. Irrespective of the verdict of scholars, will it be the fate of *The Heavenly City* to continue to attract those who like to reflect on the past and to make sense to those who share his concern about the prospects of freedom? Or has Becker inadvertently helped to nurture the New Conservative movement? These questions are treated by various contributors to this volume.

The general outline of the symposium program, an expedition, twenty-five years after publication, back to Becker's classic, has been retained in the sequence of papers in this volume. A "local affair" arranged for members of the Association, the program featured a number of well-known scholars, among whom were former colleagues and students of Becker.

The original plan to hold one session on the Enlightenment, with *The Heavenly City* as the starting point, was suggested by the Association's executive committee. Its president, Sidney Harcave of Harpur College, then re-

[23] "Henry Adams Once More," in *Everyman*, 163.

quested the writer to arrange for the meeting. The topic
selected was a natural sequence to deliberations held
by the Association on the Renaissance and on the
Seventeenth-Century Scientific Revolution the two preceding years. A critique of Herbert Butterfield's controversial *The Origins of Modern Science, 1300–1800* [24]
had been the point of departure the year before. Was it
not logical for Becker's former upstate New York colleagues to select his provocative volume as the entree to
the Age of Reason? And, perhaps, the highly successful
all-day deliberation on Vernon L. Parrington's *Main
Currents of American Thought*,[25] held at Colgate University by the New York State Association for American
Studies several years earlier, was an unconscious model
for the ultimate proportions of the Becker meeting.

Conversations held by the writer in Philadelphia with
Leo Gershoy of New York University and Robert R.
Palmer of Princeton University, who agreed to serve
as program advisers and chairmen, and with other
eighteenth-century scholars attending a national meeting were responsible for expanding the plan into an all-
day symposium. The title of the sessions, "Carl Becker's
Heavenly City Revisited Twenty-five Years After,"
emerged out of a luncheon table chat between Mr. Gershoy, Crane Brinton, Gilbert Chinard, and the writer.
Seldom have conference programs been completed with
such alacrity and genuine enthusiasm. Typical was the
response of one prospective participant: "But the more
I think about your whole session the more enthusiastic
have I become. . . . The whole subject fascinates me
very much, indeed." Unfortunately, conflicts with other

[24] London, 1949.   [25] Three vols., New York, 1927–1930.

Preface

events made it impossible to schedule the meetings at
Ithaca. Although the writer had the warm support of the
Association's president, Mr. Harcave, and the advantage
of advice from Messrs. Gershoy and Palmer, he must accept full responsibility for the design of the program:

Introduction

Comments by the Honorary Chairman, George H. Sabine,
Professor Emeritus, Cornell University

Morning General Session: "The Critique"

Chairman: Robert R. Palmer, Princeton University

Papers

Henry Guerlac, Cornell University
"Newton's Changing Reputation in the Eighteenth Century"

Peter Gay, Columbia University
"Carl Becker's Heavenly City"

Luncheon Session

Chairman: Geoffrey Bruun, author of *Europe and the French
Imperium, 1799–1814*

Speaker: Walter L. Dorn, Columbia University
"The Heavenly City and Historical Writing on
the Enlightenment"

Afternoon General Session: "The Reassessment"

Chairman: Leo Gershoy, New York University

Preface

Informal Comments by Panel Members:

Geoffrey Bruun; Willson H. Coates, The University of Rochester; Louis Gottschalk, The University of Chicago; Beatrice Hyslop, Hunter College; and Robert R. Palmer.

Dinner Meeting

Chairman: Louis Gottschalk

Speaker: Morris Bishop, Cornell University
"A Letter from Carl Becker"

Discussion from the floor, fairly general in the morning, was restricted in the afternoon for want of time. Professor Gilbert Chinard, originally scheduled to present a paper, was unfortunately unable to attend. Without the painstaking efforts of the two recorders, Ralph Greenlaw of Wellesley College and John Hall Stewart of Western Reserve University, the give and take of the meeting could not easily have been recovered for purposes of publication. Although the symposium was not arranged with the deliberate intention of seeking publication, the present volume was undertaken in response to a general and enthusiastic mandate from many people attending the sessions. The gathering of the materials, which involved considerable pressure on busy people, was aided by the chairmen of the sessions, who, nevertheless, are not responsible for the contents except for their own contributions. Special thanks are due Mr. Gershoy for his sympathetic assistance and to my friend and colleague, Jonathan Kistler, associate professor of English at Colgate University, for his help in the preparation of the manuscript.

Preface

The product of a highly informal situation designed to promote an intellectual exchange, the book is not presented as a systematic and full treatment of all possible aspects of the problem. The purpose has been to offer a variety of perspectives and to achieve a balanced, fair, and sympathetic treatment of a significant historical work. The spirit of a symposium has been maintained without reproducing all the discussion from the floor. Some statements have been revised or elaborated in the light of the proceedings. All papers were written by individuals present at the meetings.

The analysis of *The Heavenly City* opens in Part I with three papers prepared as a basis of discussion at the morning and noon sessions. Following in Part II are the remarks of various afternoon panel members revised after the event and, in some instances, considerably enlarged. The concluding section, Part III, comprises four perspectives written by participants after the event in the light of the total deliberation.

The dimensions of the case against *The Heavenly City*, established in Part I by Messrs. Guerlac, Gay, and Dorn, and in Part III by Ralph Bowen, are also developed in certain papers presented at the afternoon session. The most provocative and controversial attack, as is clearly reflected by the responses in this volume, was that of Mr. Gay, an analysis that should be compared for tone and shading of the argument with Mr. Bowen's critique. The spirit of Mr. Dorn's estimate, in which he undertakes to be "honestly critical and scrupulously fair," is a norm shared by all contributors. It is easier for those like him or Dr. Hyslop, not closely associated with Becker, to adopt a position of detachment. Whether a deep personal

Preface

involvement with the subject may in fact contribute to a more profound and sensitive appreciation and to a more genuine objectivity is a fascinating historiographical question posed by the volume. For it is evident, as is revealed by any reading of the papers by Messrs. Palmer, Gottschalk, or Gershoy, that critical judgment is scarcely a monopoly of the critics.

The impact of Becker's personality, thus cannot be escaped and is particularly evident in the assessments written by his students. Of the fourteen contributors to the present volume, six are former Becker students (Bruun, Coates, Gershoy, Gottschalk, Palmer, and Stewart) and three were intimately associated with him (Mr. Sabine as a colleague, Miss Gaskill as librarian, and Mr. Guerlac as a faculty son). Mr. Sabine's perceptive remarks in the introduction bring Becker as a person—a mentality—vividly into the deliberations. Most symbolic of the warm glow of Becker as an individual that *The Heavenly City* recalls to the minds of devoted students is Mr. Bruun's tribute to Becker's humanity.

Mr. Palmer occupies a mid-position between the critics and the supporters of *The Heavenly City*. The most vigorous defenders of Becker's work are Messrs. Gottschalk and Gershoy. Mr. Gottschalk rereads *The Heavenly City* to find it a consistent and sound expression of Becker's basic concerns. In the concluding chapter, Mr. Gershoy reviews the argument of the symposium and, in general, justifies Becker's achievement, which is explained as a phase of his intellectual development. Just preceding Mr. Gershoy's paper are two other overviews of the sessions—by Messrs. John Hall Stewart and Edward W. Fox, the latter Becker's successor at Cornell—which enable the reader to recapture the atmosphere of the meet-ing. The "magnetic deviation" of the first favors Becker. Whether Mr. Fox's portrayal is to be classified as an un-friendly attack on Becker, as a shaft directed at both sets of protagonists, or as an impressive tribute to a scholar whom he deeply admires as greater than the general run of historians—are questions not to be an-swered too hastily.

Although the reader confronts some repetition in these studies and commentaries, he is particularly impressed by the varied perspectives and approaches. Perhaps no exercise could go further in confirming Becker's judg-ment respecting the nature of historical analysis. There has been no conscious endeavor to synthesize the diverse arguments, if that were possible, or to draw conclusions. This task remains a challenge to the thoughtful reader. Above all, the journey back to Becker's *The Heavenly City* does not presume to reassess his life work. The trip was a pilgrimage from which most of the participants returned with renewed admiration tempered by a more realistic understanding of the terrain traversed. One may modestly hope that this exploration of a brief episode in Carl Lotus Becker's fruitful career does in fact open new vistas for an appreciation of one of America's truly dis-tinguished historians and teachers.

For permission to quote from copyrighted publications the editor is grateful to the following: Yale University Press for the innumerable and inevitable citations of *The Heavenly City of the Eighteenth-Century Philosophers* and for quotations from Becker's "Some Generalities That Glitter" in the *Yale Review;* Harper and Brothers, Publishers, for an excerpt from Becker's *Our Great Ex-*

Preface

periment in Democracy: A History of the United States; Alfred A. Knopf for quotations from Progress and Power and The Declaration of Independence; Princeton University Press for a passage from Ronald S. Crane, ed., English Literature, 1660–1800; Silver Burdett Company for quotations from Becker's Modern History (copyright 1931); and the Yale Law Journal for quotations from a review of Becker's The Heavenly City by Max Lerner. He wishes also to acknowledge permission to reprint Peter Gay's article, "Carl Becker's Heavenly City" granted by the Political Science Quarterly.

The editor also wishes to acknowledge with gratitude financial assistance in the final preparation of the manuscript made available by the Colgate University Research Committee from a grant to support research and writing at Colgate given by the Lucius N. Littauer Foundation, Inc.

RAYMOND O. ROCKWOOD

Colgate University
March 25, 1958

Contents

Contents

GEORGE H. SABINE

CORNELL UNIVERSITY

Introduction:

The Right to Reassessment

AFTER I was told that there was to be a conference on Carl Becker and a "reassessment" of his work as a historian, and more particularly that I had a small part to play in it, one query kept recurring to my mind: What would Becker think about it? I am certain of only two things. First, he would have taken it quite seriously, for reassessments were very much in his line. He called them "inserting a small question mark" after some favored valuation. Few historians have tried so seriously or so continuously to assess the part that their science, or their art, can and ought to play in the intellectual life of a society, and few writers on historiography have made self-consciousness—the awareness of his own presumptions—so nearly a moral obligation of the historian.

Second, I know that Becker would also have been a little amused, for his seriousness was matched by his irony, and his own reassessments were not always conducted with the solemnity sometimes thought proper to that process. A writer or a thinker who has reached the stage of being reassessed has attained something like Nirvana, and literal-minded people always find it hard to say exactly how Nirvana differs from just not being. Yet, in this curious thing called "culture," which is the distinguishing mark of human society and the peculiar capacity of the human animal, there is a kind of middle ground between being and not being—the point at which a teacher has ceased to be an entity in his own right and has become a pervasive force in the minds of another generation carrying on the never-ending enterprise. Most of you will recall the sentence in which Becker summed up his reassessment of his own teacher Frederick Jackson Turner: "For my part I do not ask of any historian more than this, that he should have exerted in his generation a notable influence upon many scholars in many branches of humanistic study." By that standard Becker has earned the right to be reassessed.

For Becker, and for most of us who try to grasp some phase of intellectual history, the fascinating and baffling aspect of the study is the transformation which a body of ideas may undergo when it is transplanted from the environment in which it grew up into a different environment to which the ideas must adapt themselves. Apart from the more abstract sciences the transformation is often in only a small degree the outcome of logic—a pursuit of internal consistency, and extension of precise implications, and the adoption into a system of new and well-authenticated facts. The terms are too vague, the words are too slippery, and the ideas are continually modified in unspecified ways by their new contexts. The historian who tries to describe or suggest what Becker called a "climate of opinion" must depend upon a faculty which is hard to control—imagination, or sympathy, or an artist's empathy—by which he reconstructs in his own mind the thoughts, but also the feelings, the values and aspirations, of the men who were the bearers of the ideas. And ideas have always to be borne by someone who is a good deal less, and a good deal more, than even the best electronic calculator. The historian's faculty of imagination is at once a necessary but a dangerous tool. There is only a fine line, or perhaps no clearly distinguishable line at all, between imagination and impressionism, between legitimate emphasis and overemphasis, between the selection which is unavoidable and the selection which overplays or underplays its similarities or contrasts. Those of us who knew Becker will not, I fancy, disagree with the statement that the quality of his own powers was that which he attributed to Jefferson: "a nature exquisitely sensitive and a mind finely tempered." But Becker himself knew that these powers are chronically in a state of internal war: the generalizations will not move forward and the concrete events will not generalize.

Becker's generation—the generation that made current Marx's baffling word "ideology"—was curiously indifferent to precision in its use of ideas and to self-contradiction. I recall a long debate at a philosophical conference in which John Dewey was the principal speaker and which reached a climax when a critic said, "It seems to me, Mr. Dewey, that you have contradicted yourself." Dewey replied with a kind of mild but not much concerned surprise, "Why, I believe I have." If he had been accustomed to use slang, he might have added, So what? Becker, too, was tolerant of inconsistency, or at least he claimed to be consistent only in terms of "certain convictions"—"prejudices, if you prefer"—which like Justice Holmes he would have said were more pervasive than any major premise.

Anyone whose reassessment of Becker takes the form of showing that he was a child of his own generation—which he would no doubt cheerfully admit—will have an easy task. In my subject the ideas of William James and John Dewey which formed the philosophical currency of that first decade of the century, when Becker adopted them as the medium of exchange for expressing his own ideas about history, have long since been taken out of circulation. Their issuance and their retirement, and the period of their use, have fallen within the span of a single lifetime. Ideas "work" no doubt, but how? What is their dependence, or their independence, on that vast reserve of circulating medium for communication, language? And are there standard values that sometimes make the medium more than a token currency? I think this change, which he might have lived to see, would have fascinated Becker, as he was fascinated by similar transformations in the ideas of other times. I am sure that he would not have been offended if his history and his historiography were said to be "dated." For this, he would have said, is the common fate of scholars. He would only have hoped that those who reassess him would do as well in their generation as he did in his, or if possible better.

PART I

The Critique

HENRY GUERLAC

CORNELL UNIVERSITY

1. Newton's
Changing Reputation
in the Eighteenth Century

FEW pieces of historical writing by American historians
of the older generation have left a more profound mark
upon our own than Carl Becker's *The Heavenly City of
the Eighteenth-Century Philosophers.* And few works
that have won this position of influence seem to demand
for their intelligent comprehension as much understanding of the author's temperament and individuality as
does this series of lectures. I knew Professor Becker far
less well than many who are contributing to this symposium; I was never his student, to say nothing of being
his colleague. Yet having grown up in Ithaca when
Becker was in his prime, I met him on numerous occasions, heard him talk, and got some feeling for the tem-

per of his mind. It is difficult for me to exclude these impressions from what I think about *The Heavenly City,* so perhaps I should begin by recalling them.

I think I met Mr. Becker first in my humble capacity as youthful cupbearer to small gatherings of historians that my father, who taught French at Cornell in Becker's time, used to assemble in his library. This group often included George Lincoln Burr, Preserved Smith, our neighbor Charles Hull, and, of course, Carl Becker. As my reward for buying and distributing the Swiss cheese and the near beer—for those were prohibition days—I was allowed to sit in a corner and listen to the talk, with firm instructions from my father to watch for emptied glasses and to maintain a proper silence. Much of the conversation turned on history, and much of it—needless to say—was beyond me. But the talk, unlike the beer, was intoxicating, even when I had difficulty following it.

What I chiefly remember of those evenings with Carl Becker—aside from the fact that he was the least loquacious of the group—was his impatience with sham and pomposity and his demonstration that even the most important matters could be said without pontification and the most thorny subject illumined by the passing insight and the ironic *aperçu.*

This is why I find my present assignment difficult and even slightly embarrassing. From what little I know of Becker I suspect he would be quietly amused to hear his *Heavenly City,* in which these characteristics are so manifest, discussed with great solemnity as if it were a pretentious monograph on the great age he relished and admired so much.

The Heavenly City, I hardly need remind you, is not

a monograph or a synthetic study but a minor masterpiece of that precious but obsolescent form of writing,
the historical essay. Whatever else we may think of it,
few would deny that it is a work of literary art—a proof
that historians can write well and need not, indeed
should not, write like sociologists. To dissect a minor
work of art—above all a work of deft irony and marked
elusiveness—with the blunt tool of scientific criticism
often seems, even when it is necessary, to be a somewhat barbarous task. And it becomes also a bit absurd
when one has the uncomfortable feeling that perhaps the
author took the work less seriously than does the critic.
So it is fair to ask, at the start, how seriously Becker took
the conclusions of *The Heavenly City,* for the book is
surely something of a *jeu d'esprit.* But even if Becker did
not take his conclusions literally, in one sense at least
I am convinced he took the book as a whole quite seriously. As a distinguished teacher—indeed, for graduate
students, one of the great teachers—Becker was well
aware how hard it is to make people *think,* especially
those historians and teachers of history who view their
task solely in terms of bibliographies and footnotes. I
suspect the chief purpose of *The Heavenly City* was to
make us think—to move us to a new vantage point
from which to contemplate some of the familiar facts
of eighteenth-century intellectual history and to shed a
beam of paradox over well-traveled ground.

Such a radical change of position is often what is
needed; and this makes me think of the M.I.T. professor
who has found that many mechanical puzzles prove in-
soluble when examined in the ordinary way but that
the solutions—or at least the elements of a problem—

reveal themselves at once if the student will only have the kindness to stand on his head. I think that Becker has, in a manner of speaking, made us stand on our heads to contemplate the Age of Reason, and in doing so he has shown us aspects we would otherwise not perceive. Yet Becker would have been the last to recommend this posture as a permanent one for *Homo sapiens,* and I think he would have been unhappy to learn that many of his readers have remained ever since in the position in which he placed them. Sad to relate, this is precisely what has happened. A generation of history students has been brought up to take *The Heavenly City* more literally than I believe Becker intended. Its paradoxes have been hardened into doctrine by a succession of textbook writers.

There is some point then in examining, as we are doing here, what Becker said, the manner of his saying it, and the conclusions that have been widely drawn from this stimulating book. I shall leave to Peter Gay, who has done the job expertly, as you shall see, the task of discussing the book as a whole. I shall limit myself to one aspect only, an important aspect, to be sure, and one that falls properly within the province of the historian of science. This is Becker's interpretation of the influence on eighteenth-century thought of what he calls—as many in that century also did—the "Newtonian philosophy."

Becker carefully placed this term in inverted commas, and he was much too wise to identify this "Newtonian philosophy" either with Newton's own discoveries and opinions or with the totality of eighteenth-century scientific thought. He is careful to speak of Newton as a convenient *symbol* of the influence of science on the world view of the Age of Reason, much as Darwin was a symbol in the great debates about the role of science that raged through the middle and late nineteenth century.[1] And he surely did not believe that the science of either period could be adequately summed up in the work and influence of a single man, however great. But our textbook writers have been unmindful of Becker's *caveat;* they have drawn from *The Heavenly City* certain persistent notions about the influence of Newton in the eighteenth century and the debt to him of the social philosophers of the Enlightenment.

What Becker says of Newton and the "Newtonian philosophy" is familiar to all of you, and I do not propose to cite him at length. Instead, I should like to set down in the form of six propositions certain ideas which I believe are widely and erroneously accepted and which appear to me to sum up the prevailing impressions concerning the place of science in the Enlightenment. Here they are:

1) That the science which interested the men of the eighteenth century was "Newtonian science," which is to say chiefly physical astronomy and cosmology.

2) That the substance of this scientific outlook was

[1] "The 'Newtonian philosophy' was, accordingly, as familiar to common men in the middle eighteenth century as the 'Darwinian philosophy' is in our day. . . . No need to open the *Principia* to find out what the Newtonian philosophy was—much better not, in fact. Leave that to the popularizers, who could find in the *Principia* more philosophy than common men could, very often more, I must say, than Newton himself did" (*The Heavenly City* [New Haven, Conn., 1932], 60–61).

derived from the discoveries and opinions set down in Newton's *Principia* of 1687.

3) That this Newtonian physics introduced men for the first time to the notion of a mechanistically determined universe of external nature and that Newton's discoveries lay behind the materialistic picture of a physical universe made up only of massy particles in motion, operating like a vast piece of clockwork.

4) That the lessons of this physics largely explain eighteenth-century man's abiding faith in the regularity of nature and the inexorableness and simplicity of the "Laws of Nature and of Nature's God."

5) That the chief writers of the Enlightenment—*philosophes* and *économistes* alike—had their world view shaped by this Newtonian philosophy; that these men were all Newtonians, in the sense that they accepted, in simplified and diluted form, the cosmological and physical assumptions of Newton's *Principia*.

6) That the *philosophes,* like their loyal readers, cared little for what was taking place in science but much for the use they could make in their liberal propaganda of this "Newtonian philosophy"; and that their knowledge of science was scanty and came largely through such Newtonian popularizers as Pemberton, Maclaurin, Algarotti, and Voltaire.

You will recognize that these propositions are deliberately oversimplified, and you will probably see that while Becker may have said some of these things, and seems to imply others, he certainly did not say them all or mean them all. Yet, without undue exaggeration, these are some of the conclusions commonly drawn from *The Heavenly City*, and we have heard them all in one form or other.

I shall return in a moment to these propositions, only stopping here to remark that they present a wholly misleading picture of the role of science in eighteenth-century thought, as any reading of Cassirer, Lovejoy, and Chinard will convince you. Today we know far more than Becker could have known, with the resources at his disposal, about this important problem. We know more about Newton himself and his accomplishments,[2] and the reputation he enjoyed in the Age of Reason. From Margaret Libby, Ira Wade, and others we have learned to take Voltaire's excursion into science more seriously than Becker did.[3] New and important studies

---

[2] See for example Florian Cajori's usefully annotated English version of the *Principia* (Berkeley, 1934) and, appearing in the same year, Louis Trenchard More's *Isaac Newton* (New York, 1934), a detailed biography. On the technical side the reader should consult the numerous contributions of Alexandre Koyré. Recent specialized studies have stressed the important influence of Newtonian thought, especially the *Opticks*, on chemistry and other branches of experimental science. See I. B. Cohen, *Franklin and Newton* (Memoirs of the American Philosophical Society, 43; Philadelphia, 1956), and my "Continental Reputation of Stephen Hales," *Archives internationales d'histoire des sciences*, IV (April, 1951), 393–404.

[3] Margaret S. Libby, *The Attitude of Voltaire to Magic and the Sciences* (New York, 1935); Ira O. Wade, *Voltaire and Madame du Châtelet: An Essay on the Intellectual Activity at Cirey* (Princeton, N.J., 1941); the same author's *Voltaire's Micromégas: A Study in the Fusion of Science, Myth and Art* (Princeton, N.J., 1950) and his *Studies on Voltaire* (Princeton, N.J., 1947), especially chap. ii, sec. 5.

have appeared on most of the great figures of the Enlightenment, and the authors have been at pains to examine the scientific interests of their subjects.[4] Diderot has been the object of intensive research, and so has the persistent influence of Cartesian thought in the course of the century.[5] And I should add that the history of eighteenth-century science is receiving increased attention from specialists in this field.[6]

[4] For example, the recent studies of Montesquieu by Pierre Barrière (1946) and Sergio Cotta (1953); Pierre Naville's *Paul Thiry d'Holbach et la philosophie scientifique au XVIIIe siècle* (Paris, 1943); Daniel J. Boorstin's *The Lost World of Thomas Jefferson* (New York, 1948); Douglas Dakin's *Turgot* (London, 1939); Carl Van Doren's well-known *Benjamin Franklin* (New York, 1938); and Paul Dimoff, *La vie et l'oeuvre d'André Chenier* (2 vols., Paris, 1936).

[5] Of importance are the papers of Herbert Dieckmann and the well-documented study by Aram Vartanian, *Diderot and Descartes: A Study of Scientific Naturalism in the Enlightenment* (Princeton, N.J., 1953). See also Paul Mouy, *Le développement de la physique cartésienne* (Paris, 1934); Robert Lenoble, *Mersenne, ou la naissance du mécanisme* (Paris, 1943); and Raymond Bayer, ed., *Etudes cartésiennes* (Paris, 1937), a collection of valuable papers presented to the IXe Congrès International de Philosophie.

[6] See the important work of the late Hélène Metzger, especially her *Newton, Stahl, Boerhaave et la doctrine chimique* (Paris, 1930); A. Wolf's encyclopedic *A History of Science, Technology and Philosophy in the Eighteenth Century* (New York, 1939); and Emile Guyénot, *Les sciences de la vie aux XVIIe et XVIIIe siècles* (Paris, 1941). There are a number of excellent special studies of scientific figures such as Pierre Brunet's *Maupertuis* (2 vols., Paris, 1929); Jean Torlais' *Réaumur* (Paris, 1936); René Taton's *L'oeuvre scientifique de Monge* (Paris, 1951); and the short but penetrating studies of French naturalists (Buffon, Daubenton, Cuvier, Lamarck, and Lacépède) by Louis Roule. The literature on Lavoisier is reviewed in my "Lavoisier and His Biographers," *Isis,* XLV (May, 1954), 51–62.

Newton's Changing Reputation

If it is not fair to judge Becker harshly from our improved position, it is nevertheless our business to ask how much use he made of materials available when he set to work to prepare these now-famous Storrs Lectures. What had he read? What could he have read?

First of all, let us remember that what Becker has to say of Newton and eighteenth-century science in *The Heavenly City* was taken, with no perceptible alteration, from the more extended treatment he had included ten years before in his *The Declaration of Independence*, where he gives one of the first accounts in English of the spread and influence of Newtonian thought in France.[7] He seems to have sought out little of significance in the intervening period. He did not tackle, or see the importance of, Ernst Cassirer's *Erkenntnis Problem*, the second volume of which would have proved illuminating. Except for the Newtonian popularizers, whom he cites with delight, he seems to have taken his general picture of eighteenth-century science largely from William Whewell's antiquated *History of the Inductive Sciences* or from the pedestrian *History of Science* of Dampier-Whetham. Although, between the two drafts, Becker encountered Whitehead's *Science and the Modern World* (1925), a book which left a strong imprint on *The Heavenly City*, he found little to cause him to alter his earlier opinions.

Yet at the time he wrote, there was already a substantial secondary literature of which he seems to have been oblivious or about which he was indifferent. The latter, I think, is probably the case, for I am not persuaded that

[7] Carl Becker, *The Declaration of Independence* (New York, 1922), 40–51.

Becker had the slightest interest in the harsh and sometimes grubby materials of the history of science. Two
important books appeared, one in the same year as *The
Heavenly City,* the other a year later, which show that
the facts were not totally inaccessible, and also that they
led to conclusions quite at variance with his own. The
first was Cassirer's *Philosophie der Aufklärung.* Little
read by historians in this country until the author arrived in person just before World War II as a refugee
from Nazi Germany, it is only now reaching a wide
audience as a result of the English translation brought
out in 1951. It is a penetrating book, by a historically
minded philosopher of great genius who was steeped in
the primary materials and the secondary literature.

A quite different sort of book was published in 1934
by Becker's colleague in the Cornell Department of History, Preserved Smith. This was the second volume of
Smith's *A History of Modern Culture.* It did not, I understand, elicit much enthusiasm from the reviewers; yet
its merits lie precisely in those chapters on eighteenth-
century science which the reviewers were least likely
to appreciate. Historians of science, and I am among
them, have often praised it. Its documentation is formidable, and Smith's conclusions, insofar as he troubled to
draw conclusions, are largely sound. If he did not penetrate as profoundly as did Cassirer into the thought of the
age, his account supplements the *Philosophie der Aufklärung* in several important respects: it conveys the
richness and variety of science in the eighteenth century;
shows that this century was by no means held in bondage
solely by the memory of Isaac Newton; [8] and, together

[8] If the second chapter of Smith's book is entitled "Newtonian
Science," the chapter following (dealing with natural history,

with the work of Daniel Mornet, convinces us that the general appreciation of science was a social and intellectual phenomenon in the eighteenth century without which the thought of the Enlightenment can scarcely be understood.[9]

Let us now consider the six propositions in the light of what is now becoming known about our problem:

1) The science which interested the men of the eighteenth century was not merely "Newtonian science," nor was it confined to physics and cosmology. Other branches of physics—like the discoveries in electricity—captured the public imagination, especially during the second half of the century. Natural history—stimulated by the work of men like Réaumur, Buffon, Bonnet, and Linnaeus—was devotedly studied and became a source of pleasure and fruitful speculation to many a painstaking collector, both noble and *roturier*.[10] The mysteries

---

geology, and biology) is significantly called "Linnaean Science"; the author makes use of Daniel Mornet's classic *Sciences de la nature en France, au XVIIIe siècle* (Paris, 1911) and of the important books of Pierre Brunet which Becker ignored: the basic *Introduction des théories de Newton en France au XVIIIe siècle* (Paris, 1931) and the no less important *Physiciens hollandais et la méthode expérimentale en France au XVIIIe siècle* (Paris, 1926).

[9] See Preserved Smith's chap. iv, "The Place of Science in Eighteenth-Century Thought."

[10] Besides the work of Mornet, the reader should consult Edouard Lamy, *Les cabinets d'histoire naturelle en France au XVIIIe siècle et le Cabinet du Roi (1635–1793)* (Paris, [1931?]). He will find useful material for the American colonies in Michael Kraus, *The Atlantic Civilization: Eighteenth-Century Origins* (Ithaca, N.Y., 1949), especially in chap. vii, "Scientific Relations between Europe and America"; and in Brooke Hindle, *The Pursuit of Science in Revolutionary America, 1735–1789* (Chapel Hill, N.C., 1956).

of reproduction—as elucidated in part by the work of Bonnet on parthenogenesis and Trembley's study of the hydra [11]—were heatedly debated in the salons as well as the laboratory. Chemistry, mineralogy, and broader geological problems, not only yielded some of the century's most important scientific accomplishments, but these advances were discussed in the periodical press, and crowded public lectures were devoted to them. In one year, for example, a popular topic of conversation was the new noble metal, platinum; a year later it was the discovery that the diamond—thought to be not only the hardest, but the most resistant, of natural substances —could be utterly destroyed by fire. The public sessions of the Academy of Sciences in Paris, held once in the spring and once in the fall, were social events of great popularity. These examples, and a casual perusal of the gazettes or of the *Encyclopédie,* should convince the most skeptical that we are dealing with a sincere, if sometimes amateurish, interest in all manner of timely scientific questions.[12]

[11] A. Vartanian, "Trembley's Polyp, La Mettrie, and 18th-Century French Materialism," *Journal of the History of Ideas,* XI (June, 1950), 259–286.

[12] When Becker writes, "What were most of the scientific academies in France doing but discussing, quarreling about, and having a jolly time over the framing of projects?" (*Heavenly City,* 40), he reveals that he has never perused the solid and technical contents of the *Mémoires* of the Royal Academy of Sciences at Paris. What he says does not even adequately describe the activities of the more amateurish provincial academies, like those of Dijon or Bordeaux. For the Academy of Dijon the reader can consult "Notes et documents pour servir à l'histoire de l'Académie des Sciences, Arts et Belles-Lettres de Dijon," *Mémoires de l'Académie,* 2ème série, t. 16 (1871), as well as Georges Bouchard's *Guyton-*

2) Insofar as there existed throughout the century such a commonly held "world view" as Becker describes under the term "Newtonian philosophy"—and a close reading of the texts does not quite bear this out—it would seem to owe as much to Descartes, and to other influences from the previous century, as it does to Newton.

3) It was certainly not Newtonian physics that first introduced thoughtful men to the notion of a mechanistically determined physical universe. This, again, was largely the work of Descartes who, more than any other philosopher or scientist, had made systematic use of this basic article of scientific faith. Still less can we lay at Newton's door the crude materialism we find in some of the later writers of the eighteenth century. This materialism drew heavily on Descartes—even when its tenets were expressed in Newtonian language—but it also derived to a surprising extent (as I have tried to show elsewhere) from classical sources, so that we may with some justice speak of a Neo-Epicurean revival among the thinkers of the second half of the eighteenth century.[13] This is an important matter if we wish to be clear about the religious implications of scientific progress in the eighteenth century. It is not from scientists (certainly not from Newton), but from philosophers, that the atheistic materialism of d'Holbach and Diderot can be legitimately and logically derived.

Morveau (Paris, 1938). For the Bordeaux Academy there is P. Barrière, *L'Académie de Bordeaux* (Bordeaux, 1951).

[13] I have expanded this point in my paper "Three Eighteenth-Century Social Philosophers: Scientific Influences on Their Thought," *Daedalus*, Winter 1958, pp. 8–24. The reader may consult Louis Bertrand, *La fin du classicisme* (Paris, 1897), for the general problem, though not as applied to science.

Henry Guerlac

Newton's physics—like that of Galileo before him—was far less materialistic and concrete than is commonly supposed and than Becker believed. Becker's strongly empiricist interpretation of the work of Galileo and Newton would hardly satisfy a modern historian of science. To describe these men as making "relatively little use" of deductive logic and as enthroning instead a technique of observation and measurement and a reliance on brute fact [14] is to distort our knowledge of the founders of modern exact science. Newton's physics was highly abstract, a true mathematical physics, dealing with idealized bodies moving in a wholly idealized time and space.

[14] *Heavenly City*, 17, 20–21. It was precisely Galileo's Platonizing rationalism and his mathematical idealism that his Aristotelian opponents found most difficult to comprehend. On this the standard works are E. A. Burtt, *The Metaphysical Foundations of Modern Physical Science* (New York, 1925) and Alexander Koyré's *Etudes Galiléenes* (Paris, 1940). But see also Koyré's "Galileo and Plato," *Journal of the History of Ideas*, IV (Oct., 1943), 400–428; also Ernst Cassirer, "Galileo's Platonism," in *Studies and Essays in the History of Science Offered in Homage to George Sarton* (New York, 1947), 279–297. If the case for Galileo's rationalism is sometimes overstated, as I believe to be the case, we can certainly no longer think, if we ever could, that Galileo derived his law of falling bodies from experiment alone or that Newton discovered the laws of motion in the solar system "by looking through a telescope and doing a sum in mathematics," as Becker rather flippantly says (*Heavenly City*, 57).

It seems clearly evident that Becker's opinions concerning the nature of seventeenth-century science are taken largely from Alfred North Whitehead's *Science and the Modern World* (New York, 1925). Professor Whitehead's view that Galileo's science was "objectivist" and "anti-intellectualist" and an expression of the "historical reyolt" was not so much a paradox as a sophisticated version of a long-popular view. This view is no longer tenable. See, for example, Alexander Koyré: "An Experiment in Measurement," *Proc. Amer. Philos. Soc.*, XCVII (April 30, 1953), 222–237.

Indeed, for his cautious use of the word "attraction" to describe the mysterious force exerted between all bodies in the universe, Newton was accused of departing from the solid ground of Cartesian materialism and of introducing ideas that were neither clear nor precise. He was even charged with introducing mysterious entities in a manner shockingly reminiscent of the Scholastics.

4) Becker was well aware, of course, that the concepts of nature and natural law have a long history and that what we encounter in the eighteenth century is a change in meaning of these venerable terms. For what he calls the ideal image of nature ("too ghostly ever to be mistaken for nature herself") which had prevailed in earlier centuries, there is substituted, according to Becker, "a more substantial image." The ideal image of nature was abandoned as a result of the recent scientific discoveries: "natural law, instead of being a construction of deductive logic, is the observed harmonious behavior of material objects."[15]

But it was certainly not to Newtonian physics, or even to Cartesian "physics" before it, that eighteenth-century man owed his faith in the simple regularity of nature. This Becker surely knew. Such a conviction had been basic to Greek science; Aristotle's great scheme of things was reared upon it; and, as Lynn Thorndike has recently stressed, the pseudo-science of astrology may have played a powerful role, from the Stoic philosophers onward, in the spread of this idea.[16] Belief in scientific law—even if the term itself was not popular until after

[15] *Heavenly City*, 54, 56–57.
[16] Lynn Thorndike, "The True Place of Astrology in the History of Science," *Isis*, XLVI (Sept., 1955), 223–278.

its use by Descartes—is at least as ancient as the related tradition of a *moral* Natural Law, although it was from the moral sphere that the term "scientific law," a conscious metaphor, was itself manifestly borrowed in the sixteenth and seventeenth centuries.[17]

What was new, as a result of the Scientific Revolution, was that these uniformities were seen to be *mathematical* in character. And if this is true, as I believe most historians of science would now agree,[18] then what took place is precisely the reverse of what Becker believed to have happened. An ideal image of nature is substituted for the crude scheme of ordered common sense which was the system of the Schools. It is manifest that the scientists of the new age, like all scientists before or since, were concerned that the principles they hit upon should be in accord with the observed behavior of nature. But now, indeed, measurement and the quantitative view of nature supplied a tool for demonstrating this accord. Yet there is a more important difference: precisely because their mathematical image of nature was an ideal one, these scientists recognized that the conformity of theory to reality had to be approximative and limiting. No projectile actually follows the ideal para-

[17] Edgar Zilsel, "The Genesis of the Concept of Physical Law," *Philosophical Review*, LI (May, 1942), 245–279.

[18] Strongly emphasized by E. A. Burtt and A. Koyré, this view is supported by Hermann Weyl in his *Philosophy of Mathematics and Natural Science* (Princeton, N.J., 1949). Wilhelm Dilthey (*Gesammelte Schriften*, II [Leipzig, 1914], 260) seems to have perceived much earlier the "constructive character" and the "Pythagoreanism" of Galileo's thought. The reader can find this interpretation summarized in Herbert Butterfield's *Origins of Modern Science* (London, 1949) and in A. R. Hall's more detailed *Scientific Revolution, 1500–1800* (London, etc., 1954).

bolic path that Galileo *deduced* from his laws of moving bodies, but under favorable circumstances it can approach it. That scientific truth is not absolute but probabilistic and asymptotic; that it begins in experience and ends there, too, after passing through the mysterious alembic of mathematical deduction, Newton expressed clearly in his *regulae philosophandi*. And many men in the eighteenth century, Voltaire among them, perceived in this the great novelty of the Newtonian philosophy and saw in the "method of analysis" a powerful critical instrument to be used against the system builders and the blind adherents of tradition, who thought of truth as unique, absolute, and perfectly attainable.

5) In their scientific activities, the *philosophes* did not confine themselves by any means to a superficial study of the Newtonian popularizers. Their interest—like the public interest—in natural science was wideranging, and they were certainly not solely concerned with science because it might supply arguments for their social, political, and religious preconceptions. They were proud of science's steady advance; it testified to the power and possibilities of the rational human mind untrammeled in its work. They saw in the *method* of science —and it is here that Newton exerted his greatest influence—an analytical instrument that could be extended into other intellectual spheres, to extinguish superstition and emancipate the human mind from traditional error.[19] They were aware also of the immense practical

[19] A significant example is the use made by Voltaire of these ideas in his assault on the iniquities of French criminal jurisprudence. This I have discussed in the paper referred to above in note 13.

possibilities of improving man's welfare through the useful applications of scientific discovery, a proposition to which the Encyclopedists were especially dedicated.[20] Above all, perhaps, they saw in the great forward strides taken by science, the strongest argument for their belief in a law of human progress.[21]

Though most of the *philosophes* can lay little claim to high scientific distinction, it is wrong to think them content to read a handful of popular books. Fontenelle, Montesquieu, Voltaire, Diderot, d'Holbach, Turgot, Thomas Jefferson, Richard Price—to mention some outstanding men of letters—had a surprising sophistication and breadth of knowledge about the science of their day. Fontenelle was, of course, for many years the official expositor of the work of his colleagues in the Academy of Sciences. Voltaire, though unable to follow Newton through the maze of his mathematics, had nevertheless a keen appreciation of Newton's basic methodology and was a surprisingly accurate judge of the epistemological position taken by Newton. Diderot studied chemistry and natural history. d'Holbach, a disciple of Lavoisier's teacher, Rouelle, wrote some of the best chemical and metallurgical articles for the *Encyclopédie*. Turgot, a close friend of the outstanding scientists, drew the best of them into the service of government when he was *intendant* and *Controlleur des Finances;* and in his cor-

[20] The Baconian influence on the Encyclopedists is well known; it permeates d'Alembert's *Discours préliminaire* and, indeed, the whole project. And see Herbert Dieckmann, "The Influence of Francis Bacon on Diderot's 'Interpretation de la nature,'" *Romanic Review*, XXXIV (Dec., 1943), 303–330.

[21] Cf. Charles Frankel, *The Faith of Reason* (New York, 1948), 143–146.

respondence with Condorcet we find him writing astutely on many current scientific controversies.[22]

And perhaps it is well to be reminded that the line between *philosophe* and scientist is often impossible to draw. There were scientists whose writings on general "philosophic" questions, whose contributions to the *Encyclopédie*, or whose activities in public life and in the service of liberal causes ought to allow us to classify them as *philosophes:* d'Alembert, Maupertuis, Joseph Priestley, Benjamin Franklin, Condorcet, and Lavoisier are familiar examples.

6) Lastly—and this is the point that has given the title to my paper—it is of some interest to realize that not all the social philosophers of the Enlightenment were Newtonians; that is, when they invoked for ideological purpose the findings of physics, it was not always the physics of Newton. While the thinkers were generally more or less loyally Newtonian in Britain and the American colonies,[23] the situation in France was more complicated. Even in professional scientific circles, the reputation of Newton, or let us say his influence, suffered some surprising changes in the course of the century.

[22] Charles Henry, ed., *Correspondance inédite de Condorcet et de Turgot* (Paris, 1883). Of especial interest are letters in which Turgot discusses the problem of the gain in weight of metals on calcination and advances—before Lavoisier—the theory that air must be the cause. I shall treat this in a forthcoming paper.

[23] There is little doubt that, as far as Britain and its American colonies were concerned, Newton was, in the words of Cotton Mather, "the perpetual Dictator of the learned World." See, for example, Clinton Rossiter, *Seedtime of the Republic* (New York, 1953), 133–135. For the influence of *Newton's Opticks* on English poets of the eighteenth century there is, of course, Marjorie Nicolson's *Newton Demands the Muse* (Princeton, 1946).

To begin with, we should remember the unchallenged influence that Descartes exerted over physical science in France during the first third of the century. This influence was remarkably persistent. Fontenelle, who remained until his death in 1757 a stanch Cartesian in physics, is not the only outstanding case. It is less fully appreciated that Montesquieu also remained loyal to Descartes, that he had little knowledge and only limited appreciation of the accomplishments of Isaac Newton, and that he did not accept Newton's System of the World.[24]

The great wave of Newtonian enthusiasm in France coincided with the battle against the dominant Cartesians: the high point of this enthusiasm was the period from about 1732 to about 1755, when it was stimulated

---

[24] Montesquieu's bias toward mechanistic (iatrophysical) physiology is well known. See my chapter "Humanism in Science," in Julian Harris, ed., *The Humanities, An Appraisal* (Madison, Wis., 1950). In his early physical papers, the *Discours sur la cause de la pesanteur des corps* (May, 1720) and the *Discours sur la cause de la transparence des corps* (August, 1720), the doctrine of attraction is not to be found, nor is there any mention of Newton except for his discovery of dispersion. Two of Montesquieu's chief scientific correspondents were Father Castel and J. J. Dorious de Mairan, both stanch anti-Newtonians. Montesquieu read with approval Castel's *Vrai système de physique de M. Isaac Newton, exposé et analysé en parallel avec celui de Descartes* (1743) and remarks that, while Newton is a great geometer, his opinions may be false and that he "auroit souvent été lu sur l'opinion de l'infaillibilité de la géométrie." ("Spicilège," *Oeuvres*, ed. Pléiade [Paris, 1947], II, 1370). On Mairan and Castel, see P. Brunet, *Introduction des théories de Newton* (Paris, 1931), chaps. ii and iii; see also Donald S. Schier, *Louis Bertrand Castel, Anti-Newtonian Scientist* (Cedar Rapids, Iowa, 1941). The Cartesianism of Montesquieu was long ago pointed out by Désiré André, *Sur les écrits scientifiques des Montesquieu* (Paris, 1880), 11 and 18–19.

by the campaign on behalf of Newton by scientists like Maupertuis and Clairaut and by the success of popularizers like Algarotti and Voltaire. This is the period from which Becker takes most of his evidence and which he would make typical of the entire century. Yet if a tradition of Newtonians of strict observance can be traced to the end of the century—from d'Alembert and Condillac to Condorcet and Lavoisier—and remained particularly strong among the professional scientists, there is nonetheless a pronounced change of mood after mid-century.

This shift is marked by a growing suspicion among scientists that too much emphasis had been placed upon mathematical ingenuity and not enough on experimentation and observation.[25] Even mathematicians such as d'Alembert begin to express their doubts. This anti-mathematical tendency, accompanied by pleas for more attention to natural history and the experimental sciences, finds a strong champion in Diderot and the Encyclopedists, but it is also reflected in a shift of focus within the Academy of Sciences itself [26] and in scientific activity generally. More attention is henceforth paid to chemistry, geology, and electrical experiments. The discoveries of Benjamin Franklin seemed to many to epitomize the new movement and justify the new emphasis. Just as Newton was the guiding star of the earlier decades, Franklin becomes in many quarters the new

[25] John Herman Randall, Jr., *The Making of the Modern Mind* (rev. ed.; Boston, New York, etc., 1940), 262–266.

[26] Suggested as early as 1766, a reorganization of the Academy was effected in 1785 to give a greater recognition to sciences like mineralogy, experimental physics, and natural history (Ernest Maindron, *L'Académie des Sciences* [Paris, 1888], 50–57).

hero. He comes close, in the second half of the century in France, to replacing Newton as the symbol of science and its importance for mankind.[27]

The drift away from Newton is clearly evident in the writings of Diderot and of d'Holbach. The "scientific materialism" of d'Holbach's *Système de la nature* owes little to Newton, toward whom he is by no means very friendly. Instead, his materialism is an odd amalgam of chemical speculation and veiled Cartesianism; and it shows a revived interest in the materialist philosophers of classical antiquity. These same influences, plus a tincture of Neo-Stoicism, are found in the scientific speculations of Diderot. Newton's thought seemed, to these men, too mathematical, too abstruse, and too clearly tied to the deism of the older generation.

And lastly, in the closing years of the century, a vociferous attack is leveled against Newton from still another quarter. It comes from those who believed that Newton had been excessively deified, that he had become the symbol of official Academic science, an authority as unquestioned as Descartes had been earlier and Aristotle before that. This overt anti-Newtonianism won little support among the qualified scientists, but it was nonetheless a force to be reckoned with. It began with Rousseau and was carried on as a sort of minor guerrilla warfare by some of Rousseau's admirers, chief among them the future revolutionaries, Marat and Brissot. In France this movement found its most systematic expression in Bernardin de Saint-Pierre's *Etudes de la nature;* and it is to

[27] Some interesting texts have been collected by Gilbert Chinard, *L'apothéose de Benjamin Franklin* (Paris, 1955).

this tradition that Goethe's scientific and anti-Newtonian writings owe a substantial debt.

I have tried, in the preceding pages, to focus on one matter that Carl Becker dealt with in *The Heavenly City* and to summarize the results of some recent work by historians of science and historians of eighteenth-century thought.

My argument has been directed less against certain misleading notions in Carl Becker's delightful and stimulating classic than against those who, I feel, have misread his intentions and have mistaken a stop sign for a declaration of martial law. If I am right that Professor Becker hoped to make us think, I can only conclude that he would be depressed by the result. The charm, lucidity, and convenient brevity of *The Heavenly City* have worked their spell. And a book he may well have intended to stimulate and provoke readers of some sophistication, already familiar with the eighteenth century, has become, for all too many inexperienced students, the only book they open on the subject.

But *The Heavenly City* has suffered a more serious fate. When Carl Becker talked playfully and irreverently about a century whose great accomplishments he valued and whose faith he shared more than he would openly concede, he could hardly have imagined the use that would be made of his remarks by the depreciators of much that he esteemed. Even Becker could not predict the trick that a drifting climate of opinion would play on him. In 1931 it seemed good sport to expose the humbug and the stereotypes of the superrationalist historian —was he perhaps thinking of his old master, James Harvey Robinson?—and almost a public service to deflate the supposed pretensions of science and its idolaters. I doubt that he would feel quite the same about it today. At least I am sure he would not have relished the fate that has made his book ready ammunition for the foes of reason and the antagonists of science.

PETER GAY

COLUMBIA UNIVERSITY

2. Carl Becker's Heavenly City[1]

This certainly isn't history. I hope it's philosophy, because if it's not it's probably moonshine:—or would you say the distinction is over subtle?
– Carl Becker, on the flyleaf of *The Heavenly City*, presented to T. V. Smith.[2]

CARL BECKER'S *The Heavenly City of the Eighteenth-Century Philosophers* was published twenty-five years ago. Its urbane and acidulous dissection of the *philosophes* has had great and lasting influence; few recent books on European intellectual history have been as widely read and as generously received. It is that rare work of scholarship that is also a work of literature—a masterpiece of persuasion that has done more to shape

[1] This essay was first published in the *Political Science Quarterly*, LXXII (June, 1957), 182–199.
[2] Quoted by Charlotte Watkins Smith, *Carl Becker: On History and the Climate of Opinion* (Ithaca, N.Y., 1956), 212.

the current image of the Enlightenment than any other book. Despite the skepticism of some professional historians, its witty formulations have been accepted by a generation of students and borrowed in textbook after textbook.[3]

When Becker delivered his lectures at the Yale Law School in 1931 and when he slightly revised them for publication, he seems to have thought of them as a *jeu d'esprit,* a collection of aphorisms and paradoxes meant to stimulate and (I suspect) to shock his audience.[4] But, as the Latin tag warns, the fate of books depends upon the capacities of the reader. And the worldly fate of *The Heavenly City* has been success—unexcelled, uninterrupted, and, I believe, unwarranted success. When it was first published, Charles Beard greeted it as a classic;[5] today *The Heavenly City* is in its tenth print-

[3] Reviews of *The Heavenly City* were almost unanimous in their praise. One notable exception was the perceptive review by Ira O. Wade in the *Journal of Modern History,* V (June, 1933), 233–235. An amusing exception was "J. A. L." in *America,* who complained that "there is a great deal about atmosphere and climate in this little book. After reading it, one feels that the professor is living in a fog" (*America,* XLVIII [Jan. 14, 1933], 365).

[4] I have heard *The Heavenly City* defended on the ground that Becker had only wanted to stimulate his auditors, to make them think and to re-examine their presuppositions. This defense amounts to the view that because the contents did not matter, the book could not have been misleading.

[5] In the *American Historical Review,* XXXVIII (April, 1933), 591. In estimating the influence of *The Heavenly City,* we must remember: first, the abundance of favorable reviews; secondly, the almost complete absence of published criticism (the tributes to Carl Becker by George H. Sabine, Leo Gershoy, and Mrs. Smith do not criticize *The Heavenly City,* and, in addition to Mr. Wade's review, the only severe remarks I have discovered are in Walter L. Dorn, *Competition for Empire* [New York and Lon-

ing; it appears prominently in bibliographies on the eighteenth century, and many a student reads no other book on the *philosophes*. It is indeed time that the book be subjected to a careful analysis.

I

"Before estimating a book it is well to read its title with care," Becker suggests, and the title of this book briefly states its central theme: the *philosophes* destroyed less well than they knew.[6] They were believers in their most skeptical moods, Christians in their most anti-Christian diatribes:

In spite of their rationalism and their humane sympathies, in spite of their aversion to hocus-pocus and enthusiasm and dim perspectives, in spite of their eager skepticism, their en-

---

don, 1940], 180, 402); thirdly, the favored comments on the book in such distinguished and popular textbooks as Leo Gershoy's *From Despotism to Revolution, 1763–1789* (New York and London, 1944), in which *The Heavenly City* is recommended as "penetrating and subtle" (329), and Mr. Gershoy's *French Revolution and Napoleon* (New York, 1941), in which he calls Becker's book "four brilliant essays on the *philosophes;* a penetrating analysis of their ideas and ideals" (539). In the widely used text by Crane Brinton, John B. Christopher, and Robert Lee Wolff, *A History of Civilization* (2 vols.; New York, 1955), *The Heavenly City* is described as "a charming series of essays, stressing the similarities between the eighteenth-century Age of Reason and the medieval Age of Faith" (II, 92). There are many other examples. [EDITOR's NOTE: The *Journal of Philosophy* also carried a critical review. See *supra*, vii–ix.]

[6] For Becker's remark, see *The Heavenly City*, 115. It has been said (and Becker himself said it jokingly) that *The Heavenly City* is not history at all but a moral tract. If it is not history at all, it should certainly not be recommended as good history.

gaging cynicism, their brave youthful blasphemies and talk
of hanging the last king in the entrails of the last priest—
in spite of all of it, there is more of Christian philosophy in
the writings of the *Philosophes* than has yet been dreamt of
in our histories. . . . I shall attempt to show that the *Philosophes* demolished the Heavenly City of St. Augustine only
to rebuild it with more up-to-date materials.[7]

Before launching upon this theme, Becker expounds
a general assumption about the relation of change to
permanence in history. There is change in history:
Thomas Aquinas and David Hume both used the word
"reason" but meant very different things by it, so that to
compare their philosophies by investigating simply what
they said about "reason" would do injustice to both.
Words persist, but their meanings change. But also there
is permanence in history: no era wholly liberates itself
from its antecedents, although its spokesmen may
proudly (or perhaps anxiously) proclaim that they have
made a complete break. Rhetoric may change while ideas
persist. Becker suggests that intellectual historians must
reckon with this dialectic of permanence and change
and must be misled neither by spurious novelty nor by
spurious persistence.[8]

This historiographical warning is the most valuable
idea in *The Heavenly City;* unfortunately, Becker fails to
heed it when he elaborates his thesis. He argues that despite the great change in the climate of opinion between
the thirteenth and eighteenth centuries the two centuries

[7] *Ibid.*, 31.

[8] I hope to expand my remarks on what I have here called
"spurious persistence" in a forthcoming article dealing with
periodization.

30

were far more closely related than would immediately appear or would be admitted by the *philosophes*. The *philosophes'* claim to be modern must therefore be discounted:

I know it is the custom to call the thirteenth century an age of faith, and to contrast it with the eighteenth century, which is thought to be preëminently an age of reason. . . . In a very real sense it may be said of the eighteenth century that it was an age of faith as well as of reason, and of the thirteenth century that it was an age of reason as well as of faith.[9]

The overriding fault of the *philosophes* was their naïveté: they "exhibited a naïve faith in the authority of nature and reason."[10]

This is to fall into the trap of what I have called spurious persistence. It is true that the medieval Catholic rationalists, of whom Thomas Aquinas was the most prominent, assigned to reason an important place in their

[9] *Heavenly City*, 8. Becker's use of the term "Climates of Opinion" as the heading to his first chapter suggests, correctly, that he relied heavily on Whitehead's *Science and the Modern World* (New York, 1925). Becker repeatedly quotes or paraphrases Whitehead's book without indicating his source—a sign not of unwillingness to give credit, of course, but of Becker's conviction that Whitehead's views are generally known and accepted. Whitehead describes the eighteenth century as the "age of reason, based upon faith" (83) and asserts that "*les philosophes* were not philosophers" (86). They were men who hated "dim perspectives" (*ibid.*). Whitehead, like Becker, appreciated the *philosophes:* he admired their humaneness, their hatred of cant and cruelty. But like Becker he did not think they were quite first-rate: "If men cannot live on bread alone," he remarks with reference to Voltaire, "still less can they do so on disinfectants" (87). All these formulations reappear in *The Heavenly City.*

[10] *Heavenly City*, 30. Becker does say that "Voltaire was an optimist, although not a naïve one" (*ibid.*, 37).

epistemologies. It is also true—and Becker's reminders are valuable—that the *philosophes* depended upon some unexamined premises which, to the extent that they were unexamined, may be called "faith."

But Becker infers far too much from this. Aquinas' rationalism was by no means as characteristic of the thirteenth century as Voltaire's empiricism was of the eighteenth century. Moreover, Becker forgets his own caution that words may be used in many different ways when he argues that "there were, certainly, many differences between Voltaire and St. Thomas, but the two men had much in common for all that. What they had in common was the profound conviction that their beliefs could be reasonably demonstrated." [11] But the point is precisely that the two philosophers differed over what constitutes reasonable demonstration. For Aquinas reasonable demonstration was deductive and definitional;[12] Voltaire derided such demonstrations as "metaphysics," as examples of the despised *esprit de système.*

Aquinas and Voltaire both believed that the powers of reason are limited, but they drew sharply different conclusions from this: for Aquinas, that which is inaccessible to human reason concerns the foundations of Christian theology. Where the light of reason does not shine, the lamp of faith supplies illumination. For Voltaire, on the contrary, that which is inaccessible to reason is chimerical. What can never be found ought not to be

[11] *Ibid.,* 8.
[12] Becker himself quotes a characteristic specimen of Aquinas' deductive method of arguing (*ibid.,* 3). Here as in many other places in the book Becker provides material for the refutation of his case.

sought; it is the realm not of the most sacred, but of the most nonsensical—that is, of "metaphysical" speculation. Where the light of reason does not shine, man must console himself with that philosophical modesty so characteristic of Voltaire's heroes, Newton and Locke. While Aquinas could make categorical statements about the nature of the soul, Voltaire proudly proclaimed his ignorance in such matters. In seeking to show that "the underlying preconceptions of eighteenth-century thought were still, allowance made for certain important alterations in the bias, essentially the same as those of the thirteenth century," [13] Becker thus unjustifiably plays with the word "reason."

Becker plays the same verbal game in his assertion that both centuries were centuries of faith. The word "faith" usually serves to describe two rather different psychological processes. Thirteenth-century faith (if I may simplify a complex matter) was submission, not necessarily to what was absurd, but to what was beyond proof and, after a certain point, beyond argument. Failure to have faith (as Voltaire put it facetiously) led to burning in this world and in the next. Eighteenth-century faith in reason, while perhaps often naïve, should be designated by the more neutral term "confidence." Its affirmations were public, open to examination and refutation. "Faith in reason" meant simply that for the *philosophes* the method of reason (strictly speaking the scientific method of such natural philosophers as Newton) was superior to other methods of gaining knowledge; it was superior to revelation, authority, tradition,

[13] *Ibid.*, 31.

because it was more reliable.[14] In Diderot's pornographic novel, *Les bijoux indiscrets*, there is a charming dream: the dreamer sees himself transported into a building that has no foundations and whose columns rise into the mists. The crowds walking in and around the building are crippled and deformed old men. It is the land of hypothesis, and the cripples are the makers of systems. But there is a vigorous small child, growing into a giant as the dream progresses, who draws near the fantastic building and destroys it with one blow. That giant is Experiment—no dweller of the heavenly city. Did not the *philosophes,* in their reveries, see themselves as that giant? And did they not include thinkers like Aquinas among the lame makers of systems? To denounce the *philosophes* for having faith in reason may be witty, but the paradox solves no problems in intellectual history.

Near the end of the first chapter, Becker adduces evidence to buttress his thesis. But the evidence is unsatisfactory. It is embodied in a dozen-odd generalizations designed to contrast the anti-Christian ideology of the *philosophes* with their real beliefs and premises, which were Christian or at least greatly indebted to Christianity: "If we examine the foundations of their faith, we find that at every turn the *Philosophes* betray their debt to medieval thought without being aware of it."

[14] I do not wish to assert that the *philosophes* were always consistent or thorough-going empiricists. Rousseau, who showed his respect for empirical knowledge in books III and IV of the *Contrat social* and in the other late political works, could write in the *Discours sur l'inégalité,* "Let us begin by laying facts aside, since they do not affect the question." But he was seeking to elucidate the foundations of morality, and if he did not ask a factual question he was not, after all, seeking a factual answer.

34

Becker's generalizations are indefensible not because they are too general—most generalizations are—but because some of them are inadequately explored, some are misleading, and others are simply wrong.

"They denounced Christian philosophy," Becker begins, "but rather too much, after the manner of those who are but half emancipated from the 'superstitions' they scorn." This sentence contains an important truth: the *philosophes* were venturing into territory that was largely unexplored, or had not been explored for many centuries, and they were often appalled at their own daring. However, the recurring discussions of the need for a social religion for the masses suggests not that the *philosophes* were "but half emancipated from the 'superstitions' they scorn" but, rather, that they were afraid sometimes of the social consequences of their emancipation. It is the substance of their opposition to Christianity, not the shrillness of their attacks upon it, that matters: much of the *philosophes'* vehemence can be explained by what they considered to be their mission. They were determined to expose *l'infâme* loudly, repeatedly, insistently, unsparingly, until that large public which was tepidly Christian had been won over to the new ideas.

"They ridiculed the idea that the universe had been created in six days, but still believed it to be a beautifully articulated machine designed by the Supreme Being according to a rational plan as an abiding place for mankind." True, but why "but"? There is nothing essentially Christian about this idea of "cosmos"—it had been the foundation of Stoic philosophy. There is nothing essentially Christian about this idea of God as architect

35

—the watchmaker argument for the existence of God, a favorite with the *philosophes,* appears prominently in the discourses of Epictetus. The beautifully articulated machine of the *philosophes* is not a Christian but a pagan machine. What is remarkable is not the supposed resemblance of this machine to Christianity but its always implicit and often explicit repudiation of miracles: God acts through general and uniform laws alone. Here as elsewhere Becker exploits parallels or similarities or correspondences between Christian and *philosophe* thought to claim that the two are identical or that, at the least, the latter is the direct descendant of the former. This has as much logical merit as the assertion that, since Calvin was a determinist and d'Holbach was a determinist, d'Holbach was a Calvinist.

"The Garden of Eden was for them a myth, no doubt, but they looked enviously back to the golden age of Roman virtue, or across the waters to the unspoiled innocence of an Arcadian civilization that flourished in Pennsylvania." Becker is doubtless right—a mood of nostalgia for the past or for an unspoiled civilization pervaded Enlightenment thought. But this nostalgia is not merely a substitute for the Christian state of innocence: Roman virtue, Tahitian simplicity, Chinese wisdom, and Quaker pacifism provide worldly standards. They are standards, moreover, which helped the *philosophes* to evade the censorship in the *ancien régime.* Voltaire's England, Diderot's Tahiti, Montesquieu's Persia are not simply utopias; they are indirect indictments of France.

"They scorned metaphysics, but were proud to be called philosophers." True again, but it is hard to see what this sentence proves. A philosopher is a man who loves knowledge, and when he rejects authority, revelation, system making, he may argue that in his empiricism he is the only *true* philosopher, while his forerunners were idle dreamers. This may be a justified or an unjustified claim, but it does not make the *philosophes* Christians.

"They dismantled heaven, somewhat prematurely it seems, since they retained their faith in the immortality of the soul." Damaging if true, but it is largely false. Montesquieu did not believe in the immortality of the soul, nor did Diderot, nor Hume, nor Helvétius, nor d'Holbach. Voltaire was far from unequivocal about immortality.[15] Rousseau "retained his faith," or rather claimed that he must believe in order to survive: his was a desperate personal need, by no means representative of the *philosophes*.

"They discussed atheism, but not before the servants." [16] This remark is patently derived from an anecdote told about Voltaire: one evening at supper (runs this story of doubtful authenticity) Voltaire interrupted his guests Condorcet and d'Alembert, who were voicing doubts of the existence of God, and sent the servants out of the room. "Continue your attack, gentlemen," Voltaire said after the three *philosophes* were alone. "I do not want my throat cut or my money stolen tonight." Two comments may be made on this anecdote: most of the *philosophes* of the early generation were not atheists,

---

[15] He said more than once that while the case for immortality had not been proved, the contrary had not been proved either. I think that Voltaire did not believe that the soul survived the body.

[16] Becker's statements about the *philosophes* in this and the six preceding paragraphs are in *The Heavenly City*, 30–31.

never claimed to be atheists, and only "discussed atheism" in order to refute it. This did not make them Christians, since their deism was a philosophical doctrine more than once removed from Christianity. Moreover, this anecdote does not concern religion as religion but religion as a social policeman. Whether the uneducated masses needed a supernatural religion to keep them under control was much debated in the Enlightenment, but surely this was a most utilitarian, a most un-Christian debate.

II

In the second chapter of *The Heavenly City*, "The Laws of Nature and of Nature's God," Becker seeks to show that the *philosophes* belonged to the natural law tradition, that natural law is a significant link between the Christian and Enlightenment climates of opinion, but that the *philosophes* failed to recognize this link.

Becker rightly reminds us that the *philosophes* were not cynics; that their negations were far less important than their affirmations; that they were enthusiastic projectors, reformers, moralists; that their confidence in their ability to penetrate into the mysteries of the universe and to prescribe effective remedies for social ills was often exaggerated and sometimes naïve. The *philosophes* might not admit it, but their "childlike faith" was fundamentally Christian: the *philosophes* were the "secular bearers of the Protestant and Jansenist tradition"; their programs for peace and brotherhood were inspired by "the Christian ideal of service"; the words they coined—*bienfaisance, humanité*—were meant to "express in

38

secular terms the Christian ideal of service." And this "childlike faith" was shared by nearly all the *philosophes:* "In the eighteenth century the words without which no enlightened person could reach a restful conclusion were nature, natural law, first cause, reason. . . ." And again: "Nature and natural law—what magic these words held for the philosophic century." This was the *philosophes'* true faith in reason: that they could read God's purposes in the book of nature and that natural law expressed those purposes. "This is the new revelation, and thus at last we enter the secret door to knowledge." [17]

It is difficult to sort out what is true and what is false in this plausible account. I have suggested that the *philosophes* were not free from naïveté, but that is all, I think, that should be conceded. Historians and political theorists know that the natural law tradition is infinitely complex; to draw a map of its growth, its multiple ingredients, its changing modes and varied influence, would be like drawing a map of the Nile Delta. Becker does nothing to clarify and a great deal to confuse the matter by lumping together, in the same paragraph and sometimes even in the same ironic exclamation, natural law and the appeal to nature. The appeal to nature, as Becker himself tells us with engaging candor, has been employed by most schools of thought. He mentions a most miscellaneous crew of thinkers, from Aristotle and Marcus Aurelius to Calvin, Montaigne, and Pascal. He might have added Burke, the great adversary of the *philosophes.* To say, then, that the *philosophes* appealed to nature is to say that they used this word to embody the standard by which they could judge existing insti-

[17] *Ibid.*, 46, 42, 41, 39, 47, 51.

Peter Gay

tutions, morals, and forms of government. They were doing what most of their predecessors had done, and what most of their successors would do. What is notable about the Enlightenment, as Ernst Cassirer reminds us, is that "it returns again and again to the persistent problems of philosophy." [18]

The natural law tradition is much narrower than this appeal to nature. Becker's rather superficial discussion of natural law is based on two assumptions, neither of which is tenable. He suggests that natural law is essentially Christian. But natural law had originated with the Stoics and, in a less systematic form, with the Greeks. With the writings of Justus Lipsius and Grotius in the early seventeenth century natural law was beginning to strip off its Christian associations—witness Grotius' celebrated assertion that nature would be orderly even if God did not exist. Christian natural law, even at its

[18] *The Philosophy of the Enlightenment* (Princeton, 1951), 234. Even if we admit for the sake of argument that the *philosophes* had taken the materials of their philosophy from Christianity alone, what matters for the historian of ideas is that they transformed these Christian ideas. "Grace was translated into virtue," writes Becker in *The Heavenly City*, 49. Is that not a significant translation? The *philosophes* "had only given another form and a new name to the object of worship: having denatured God, they deified nature" (*ibid.*, 63). Only? But the fact is that the sources of Enlightenment thought must not be sought in Christianity alone. When Becker writes, "A distinction between good and bad! Not a novel idea, certainly; on the contrary, a very old, a most Christian idea" (*ibid.*, 86), he might well have substituted the word "Stoic" for "Christian." The relation of Stoicism to Enlightenment thought needs further elucidation: Stoicism entered modern philosophy not only directly, through the works of Marcus Aurelius and others, but indirectly, through the Stoic elements in Christian philosophy.

40

most rationalist in Aquinas' systematic theology, is part of a complex of laws (eternal, divine, natural, and human) all of which depend upon the wisdom of God. Modern natural law is secular, "profane," autonomous. Moreover, Becker neglects the fact that many *philosophes* were reaching beyond even this secular natural law. Diderot still employed the conception of *droit naturel*, Vattel still carried on the seventeenth-century tradition of the natural lawyers, but other *philosophes*, following out the implications of British empiricism, were rejecting the natural law arguments in favor of utilitarianism. Inevitably, there was much ambivalence and uncertainty concerning natural law in this time of transition.[19] But far from being uniform disciples of any natural law doctrine, the *philosophes* were providing a bridge to nineteenth-century utilitarianism and historicism. Bentham and Hegel are the philosophical heirs of Hume and Turgot: it is this real continuity between the eighteenth and nineteenth centuries that Becker neglects in favor of a fancied continuity between the Enlightenment and Christianity.[20]

[19] Voltaire is perhaps the best example of this ambivalence. He continues to affirm the existence of natural law but is uneasy with it. As an empiricist, as a disciple of Locke's philosophic "modesty," as a caricaturist of the *esprit de système*, he is driven to doubt the existence of a law in which he would like to believe. He solves the dilemma (unsatisfactorily) by arguing that there is empirical proof for the existence of a universal, uniform law of nature.

[20] Once again Becker can be quoted on the other side of his own argument. He describes eighteenth-century natural law: "Instead of being a construction of deductive logic [it] is the observed harmonious behavior of material objects." "This," he says truly, "was a new kind of 'law of nature'" (*ibid.*, 57). But he fails to draw the necessary inferences from these observations.

41

Finally, Becker fails to distinguish between natural law as rhetoric and natural law as conviction: while most of the time he does not take the *philosophes* seriously enough, he takes their rhapsodic paeans to natural law too seriously. The *philosophes* were, above all, practical social reformers, and through their rhetoric we can sense their impatience to get to work. When Voltaire affirms that some moral rules are universally accepted and that this proves the existence of natural law, when Voltaire says briskly that "a day suffices for a sage to know the duties of man," he seems to be saying to his reader: "You and I know what is wrong in this society; you and I know what evils must be rooted out and what institutions must be changed; to split hairs about the fundamentals of morals is to escape responsibility, to substitute talk for action." [21] Social reform in the first half of the eighteenth century rested on philosophic positions no longer fully convincing even to its most fiery proponents. In overlooking this gap between talk and action, in taking the rhetoric of the *philosophes* as a literal transcription of their deepest convictions, Becker, while claiming to penetrate to fundamentals, only too often confines his analysis to the surface.

What then has become of Becker's thesis that the *philosophes* did not know what they were doing and were rebuilding the old heavenly city, only with new materials? Without wishing to be paradoxical for the sake of paradox, let me suggest that Becker's formulation

[21] I do not have sufficient space to justify in detail my contention that Voltaire's advocacy of natural law was chiefly rhetorical. I refer the reader to my forthcoming study of Voltaire's political ideas.

turns the truth upside down: the *philosophes* knew exactly what they were doing; they were building a new, earthly city. And in building it they used, along with much new material, some of the old Christian bricks. Far from being less modern than they knew, they were even more modern than they claimed.

III

Becker's analysis of natural law is unphilosophical; his analysis of the relation of the *philosophes* to history is unhistorical. That does not make it any the less delightful: in the last two chapters Becker catches, with superb wit, a certain mood of the *philosophes*. His deft characterization of Madame Roland weeping that she was not born a Roman, of Robespierre apostrophizing posterity; his apt quotation from Diderot, *"La postérité pour le philosophe, c'est l'autre monde de l'homme religieux"*— all these almost convince us that this antienthusiastic century was crowded with enthusiasts. As Becker says, the *philosophes'* aversion to enthusiasm was itself an enthusiasm.[22]

But—like Voltaire's Zadig (and, for that matter, like Becker himself) we are compelled to say "but" once again—while Becker's insights into the character of the *philosophes* are valuable, they are marginal rather than central, and Becker places too heavy a load upon his evidence.

Let me summarize his case: the sensationalism of the *philosophes*, first explored by Locke and extended by his disciples, was at first a heady and later a frightening

[22] *Heavenly City*, 37.

prospect for them. If Locke was right, there was no total depravity. But if nature was good, whence evil? "How then could Philosophers say that all was somehow good in God's sight unless they could also say that there was no evil to be observed in the world of nature and man?" Pure reason confronted the *philosophes* with "an ugly dilemma, emerging from the beautiful promises of the new philosophy," and in order to escape this dilemma they turned from reason to history. "They found . . . that reason is amenable to treatment. They therefore tempered reason with sentiment, reasons of the heart that reason knows not of; or held in leash by experience, the universal judgment of mankind. . . ." Becker professes to observe a change of temper and ascribes it to fear. "The Philosophers *began to* cold-shoulder abstract reason. . . ." "The age of reason had scarcely run half its course before the Philosophers *were admitting* the feebleness of reason, *putting the ban on* flippancy, and *turning to* the study of useful, that is to say, factual, subjects." And Becker claims to see this historical development in the works of some of the leading *philosophes*, above all in Hume: "Hume's *turning away from* speculation to the study of history, economics, and politics was symptomatic of a certain change in the climate of opinion. . . ." [23]

[23] *Ibid.*, 67, 69, 69–70, 83, 84, my italics. Becker qualifies his case at one point: "I would not leave the impression that the Philosophers began to cold-shoulder abstract reason merely, or chiefly, because they found a logical dilemma in the path; still less that they embraced the cause of virtue with greater emotional warmth because they could find no ultimate reason for embracing it at all. There may be something in all that—I am inclined to

It is doubtless fruitful to divide the Enlightenment into two periods. In the first half of the century the *philosophes* were an embattled and socially inferior group; in the second half of the century they were confident that they were winning the contest for public opinion and social prestige. In the first half of the century the rhetoric of natural law had still been prevalent; in the second half it was largely supplanted by utilitarianism. But for Becker's division—the shift from pure reason to reason softened by sentiment, from nonhistorical reason to historical reason—there is little convincing evidence. Diderot, in many respects the most representative of the *philosophes,* celebrated the passions in his earliest writings; Vauvenargues, one of Voltaire's favorite writers, warned against separating the intellect from the sentiments; Hume, developing his epistemology in the 1730s, gave the sentiments the precedence over reason.

Similarly, it cannot be shown that the *philosophes* "turned to" history because they were afraid of the implications of their godless rationalism. They wrote history as they wrote everything else: as men of letters they thought of history as a branch of literature. Voltaire wrote history—and very good history—as early as 1727–1728, when he began his *Histoire de Charles XII,* and his other historical masterpieces were conceived and probably begun in the 1730s. Nor is there the slightest evidence that the *philosophes* became more, rather than less, cautious: indeed, their daring grew with their suc-

---

think that there is; but I do not wish to make too much of it" (*ibid.,* 83). But having said that he does not wish to make too much of it, he proceeds to make too much of it.

45

cesses. Deism was characteristic of the first half of the eighteenth century; a far bolder atheism was, if not characteristic, prevalent in the second half.[24]

Why should Becker have discovered a shift in the Enlightenment that did not exist? I suspect that he needed the shift to account for the *philosophes'* solution of their moral dilemma—how to explain evil in the face of an all-good nature. But the dilemma is as imaginary as its solution. Becker does well to remind us that the *philosophes'* contribution to theodicy was unimpressive. Perhaps, if God becomes unimportant, it becomes equally unimportant to justify him. The *philosophes* viewed nature as good but not as omnipotent: Rousseau was not the only one who held that human institutions could

[24] Becker's sketch of the *philosophe*-frightened-by-his-own-temerity-and-afraid-to-undermine-morality is incorrect in many details. Becker makes much of Hume's refusal to publish his masterly and radical *Dialogues concerning Natural Religion* and attributes this refusal, chiefly, to the fact that Hume "took no pleasure in being regarded as the cold and finished skeptic, a destroyer of illusions. He was much more ambitious 'to be esteemed a man of virtue than a writer of taste'; and the fact that his history won for him the popularity he craved naturally confirmed him in his belief that it was useless to search into 'those corners of nature that spread a nuisance all around'" (*Heavenly City*, 77–78). But the fact is that Hume was extremely eager to publish the *Dialogues* and had to be strongly dissuaded by his friends, notably Adam Smith. And Adam Smith was not afraid that Hume would destroy morality but that he would get into trouble. In the last year of his life Hume revised the *Dialogues* once again and changed his will several times to make sure that they would be published after his death (since he was too ill to see them through the press himself) and published without being emasculated. See Norman Kemp Smith, Introduction, Appendix C, *Hume's Dialogues concerning Natural Religion* (2d ed.; Edinburgh, 1947), 87–96. Becker's account of the development of Voltaire's philosophy is equally unconvincing.

deprave man, that goodness could be thwarted, and that the original intentions of God could be perverted.[25] The *philosophes'* affirmation that man is by nature good does not mean that they could not account for the existence of evil, and Becker's case (that to the Enlightenment writers history provided a standard which philosophy had destroyed) falls to the ground.

While Becker rightly rejects the nineteenth-century charge that the Enlightenment was unhistorical, he accepts the charge that Enlightenment history was not "real" history but ideology. The Enlightenment historians

start out, under the banner of objectivity and with a flourish of scholarly trumpets, as if on a voyage of discovery in unknown lands. They start out, but in a very real sense they never pass the frontiers of the eighteenth century, never really enter the country of the past or of distant lands. They cannot afford to leave the battlefield of the present where they are so fully engaged in a life-and-death struggle with Christian philosophy and the infamous things that support it—superstition, intolerance, tyranny.[26]

[25] See Voltaire's little-known story, *Songe de Platon,* in which he portrays the world as created by a minor angel who made it as good as he could—which is far from perfect. In their moral and religious writings the *philosophes* sought to discredit the Christian doctrine of the fall of man, and their use of nature did not deprive them of a standard by which actions and institutions could be judged. It is only in the Marquis de Sade's perverted version of naturalism that we find the notion that nature speaks only in one voice and that everything possible or even imaginable is "natural." This is an interpretation of "natural" that the *philosophes* would never have accepted or even understood.

[26] *Heavenly City,* 105.

Peter Gay

Becker is equally harsh on nineteenth-century historians. The *philosophes,* he argues, wrote history in order to change society; the nineteenth-century historians wrote history in order to keep society as it was.[27] His criticism of historians is therefore not one-sided. But it implies either that "objective" history is impossible or that the *philosophes* fell short of writing good history. It was surely the first of these implications that Becker intended to stress, but it is the second that others have stressed in their disparagement of the *philosophes.*

I do not want to enter into the debate on the possibility of objective history here. I only want to point out that the criticism of Enlightenment historians can be overdone. Montesquieu, Voltaire, Hume, Robertson, Gibbon, wrote better histories than their present-day reputations would indicate. Becker quotes two juicy morsels: "Mankind are so much the same, in all times and places, that history informs us of nothing new or strange in this particular. Its chief use is only to discover the constant and universal principles of human nature." Thus David Hume. "History is only a pack of tricks we play on the dead." Thus Voltaire, and it is easy to see why this should have been one of Carl Becker's favorite quotations. But if we look at Hume's history of England instead of this pronouncement on history, if we look at Voltaire's masterpieces instead of this *bon mot* about history, we are impressed by their scrupulous concern for truth, their careful sifting of evidence, their intelligent selection of what is important, their keen sense of drama, their grasp of the fact that a whole civilization is a unit of study. What if Becker had quoted from the opening pages of the *Siècle*

[27] *Ibid.,* 95–97.

de Louis XIV, or from some of Voltaire's and Hume's correspondence about their historical works? These quotations might not have been as amusing or as telling as the words Becker actually quoted, but they might have been far more revealing about eighteenth-century histories.

It is perhaps a reflection of how intent Becker was to debunk Enlightenment historians that he makes a significant mistake.

The Philosophers felt that Montesquieu was too much enamored of facts as such to treat certain facts as harshly as they deserved, and it shocked them to see him dallying lightly with episodes that were no better than they should be. Voltaire (Voltaire of all people!) criticized Montesquieu for his *levity.*

The *Esprit des lois* "left a bad taste in the mouths of the Philosophers because Montesquieu insisted that the 'constant and universal principles of human nature' were after all 'relative.' " [28] The opposite is true: Voltaire and other *philosophes* admired Montesquieu but criticized him because he was a proponent of the *thèse nobiliaire,* a defender of the privileged *parlements.* They criticized him, in a word, because he was a conservative, and not because he was a relativist. Voltaire criticized Montesquieu, too, for being slipshod in his research, for accepting improbable travelers' tales—not for being "too much enamored of facts as such" but for being too little enamored of facts as such. When Voltaire (and why not Voltaire of all people?) accused Montesquieu of levity, he was referring to Montesquieu's gullibility.[29]

[28] *Ibid.,* 100–101.

[29] For Voltaire's appreciation (inadequate) and criticisms (excessive) of Montesquieu, see esp. *Commentaire sur l'Esprit des*

IV

But it is not mistakes such as these that really disappoint the reader in this charming book; the disappointment is, I think, more profound. *The Heavenly City*, as I have said, begins with a significant truth: history is concerned with the dialectical struggle between persistence and change. The eighteenth century is a century in which this struggle becomes peculiarly dramatic and complex, and the opportunities for fruitful research are great. Becker rightly urges the reader to ask searching questions, but he continually suggests the wrong answers. He argues for persistence where there was change, and he argues for one kind of persistence when there was really another.

The *philosophes* lived in an epoch in which the vitality of Christianity was waning and in which natural science, the centralized state, the development of industrial capitalism, imposed the need for a new world view. In building their earthly city, the *philosophes* fashioned their materials from the most varied sources: Christianity, a revived Stoicism and Epicureanism, and a pragmatic recognition of the needs of the new state and the new economy. In their battle for liberation from the old standards and in their search for new standards they experienced the difficulties that any individual struggling for autonomy must face. They contradicted themselves; they failed to see all the implications of their ideas; they sometimes used old words to describe new things; they some-

---

lois; Questions sur l'Encyclopédie, article "Loix, esprit des"; *Pensées sur le gouvernement;* and *L'A,B,C.*

times used rhetoric that was inappropriate to their ideas. All these questions *The Heavenly City* resolves—wrongly, I believe—with the too simple formula of its title.

The failure of the book is all the more paradoxical in view of Becker's own position. His criticisms of the *philosophes* were from the inside; as Leo Gershoy has said, Carl Becker "had always remained a believer at heart. . . . He had rejoined Voltaire and Condorcet and Wells and all the goodly company who wished humanity well." [30] But in his impatience with his intellectual forebears—an impatience which is always so much greater with those whom you admire than with those you detest —he portrayed the *philosophes* as naïve and as a little fraudulent. Becker was no conservative, but the conservative implications of *The Heavenly City* are plain.

And *The Heavenly City* failed in another, and even more paradoxical, way—through its success. Carl Becker dedicated *Everyman His Own Historian* to those who had assisted him in clarifying his ideas, "chiefly by avoiding the error of Hway, a pupil of Confucius. Hway, said Confucius, is of no assistance to me; there is nothing that I say in which he does not delight." In the twenty-five years that the book has been before the public, the error of Hway has not been avoided. It is time we admitted that Carl Becker's critique of the *philosophes,* like Samuel Johnson's critique of Shakespeare, had every virtue save one, the virtue of being right.

[30] Introduction, in Carl Becker, *Progress and Power* (New York, 1949), p. xxxvii.

WALTER L. DORN

COLUMBIA UNIVERSITY

3. *The Heavenly City* and Historical Writing on the Enlightenment

BY common consent Becker's *The Heavenly City* is one of the most remarkable specimens of historical literature to have issued from the pen of an American historian in recent decades. Indeed, its perfection of literary form and structure, its urbane and skeptical wisdom, its graceful and skillful dialectics, its spirited and engaging irony, its sovereign and easy mastery of materials, not to mention its sustained dramatic tension, give to this slender volume of lectures a literary value that is quite independent of any judgment among professionals on the merits of its argument. Where in the whole vast body of literature on the eighteenth century from Leslie Stephen, through John Morley and Kingsley Martin, down to Isaiah Berlin; from Gustave Lanson and Marius Roustan, through Daniel Mornet and René Hubert, down to Paul

Hazard; from Wilhelm Dilthey and Ernst Troeltsch down to Ernst Cassirer, will you encounter a sprightlier, less ponderous, more delightfully readable study in intellectual history than *The Heavenly City* now in its tenth printing?

After twenty-five years *The Heavenly City* still remains the unique and personal book it was when it was first published. It fits into no traditional category. It is neither a systematic study, nor even a history by orthodox standards. Even to call it a historical critique of certain aspects of the Enlightenment is scarcely adequate. On a first rapid reading one gains the impression that Becker here, with his backward glance at Thomist theology and his forward look at the high-powered industrial society of the future in which there will be less freedom and more control, intends to carry historical thinking to a higher power. In this sense *The Heavenly City* might be regarded as a rigorous exercise in the lofty detachment of a liberal but skeptical and relativist historian who proposes to demonstrate a favorite theme, the remarkable historical continuity of basic human values through the ages of revolutionary change. If Lord Acton's remark that "the higher history is the record of the abiding" is correct, then Becker's *The Heavenly City* is higher history. But whatever it is, this critique of the roots of liberalism by an outstanding liberal was provocative and was intended to be provocative. Coming from Carl Becker, already affectionately known as the American twentieth-century *philosophe,* from one whose personal values, despite his skepticism and relativism, were deeply rooted in the Enlightenment, *The Heavenly City* took his generation by surprise.

Those who discussed this nimble-witted book in print were quick to concede its originality and power. Although some of them had a vague inkling that something about this book was amiss, most of them followed the advice of Quintilian, "Do not argue with Cicero lest you come off second best." Indeed, the literary charm of the book was compelling and its argument was not too monstrous so that it was possible even for the surprised and unfriendly reader to prostrate his critical intelligence before its plausible dialectics. What was obvious was that the traditional view, that the age of the Enlightenment signified a sharp breach in the evolution of Western thought, inaugurating, as it did, the age of secularism and science, did not satisfy Becker. Yet he did not squarely challenge the validity of this view. Moreover, his studied avoidance of technical terminology resulted in a disconcerting lack of precision. Many readers could not suppress the feeling that, if there are weasel books as there are weasel words, this surely was one of them. Yet, even the critical reader, whenever he fancied he had caught the author off his guard, in an outrageous paradox, an exaggeration, or a perverse proposition, found that somewhere down the line it was usually set right. The apparently contradictory strands of argument in the book can usually be reconciled by the sympathetic reader —but it requires a very sympathetic reader.

Far more serious is the other question—whether Becker permitted his momentary pessimism over the predicament in which old-fashioned liberalism found itself in the early thirties when it pendulated irresolutely between conservatism and socialism, when he himself was prepared to entertain the thought that this liberalism had outlived its usefulness, to be reflected in *The Heavenly City* which he was then writing? Even the most sympathetic admirer of Becker must answer this question in the affirmative. Certainly it is true that there are passages in this book which become fully intelligible only if we accept the fact that at the time Becker's faith in reason, never dogmatic, was faltering. Thus, when he described modern logic as a "hocus-pocus designed to give formal validity to the conclusions which we are willing to accept," the hostile critic could say that he was coming dangerously near to denying the possibility of objective knowledge.[1] Again when in his discussion of Diderot and Hume he indicated that after the bankruptcy of religion there followed the bankruptcy of reason, when, quoting Aristophanes, he stated, "Whirl was king, Zeus having been deposed," Becker seemed to be taking an extreme relativist position.[2] Indeed, was Becker not taking an extreme relativist position when he stated that "all historical writing, even the most honest, is unconsciously subjective, since every age is bound, in spite of itself, to make the dead perform whatever tricks it finds necessary for its own peace of mind?"[3] It would seem that only the most uncritical defender of Becker would deny this. There is abundant evidence that serious critical readers, among them not only historians but philosophers, did in fact so interpret his position. That Becker later modified the position he took in *The Heavenly City* is equally certain. We know, happily, from Becker's discussion of Maurice Mandelbaum's *The Problem of Historical Knowledge* (1938) that he did believe in the possibility of objective knowledge—to be sure, within limits—

[1] *Heavenly City*, 25.   [2] *Ibid.*, 15.   [3] *Ibid.*, 44.

and that all extreme forms of relativism were thoroughly repugnant to him.[4]

Nonetheless, Becker now accorded to the Enlightenment scarcely the dignity of a halfway station between medieval Christianity and the truly modern temper and outlook, and he identified this "modern climate of opinion" with his own hard-fisted scientific naturalism or with that emergent evolutionary naturalism with which Bertrand Russell was then displaying such an obvious sympathy; at the core of both philosophic positions stands the contention that the claims of rationalism have been grossly exaggerated. That, by establishing this identity and beginning an entirely new period in the history of thought with it, Becker was being very much his own historian, he was, of course, thoroughly aware. But when he bracketed Voltaire, Volney, and St. Thomas together because they believed in a rational and orderly universe, whereas he himself found no order either in nature or in man and both, he believed, were doomed by the second law of thermodynamics, he was actually booting into the Middle Ages all moderns who believed in a rational universe, a breed which, after all, is not entirely extinct. To be sure, Becker was careful enough not to say that Voltaire had more in common with St. Thomas than with a modern philosopher like Bradley, but he did say that in fundamentals they agreed. Becker here not only underestimated St. Thomas as a philosopher but ignored the whole vast body of modern literature on religious philosophy. He was needlessly severe on such a thoroughly modern spirit as Robert Leet Patterson, who, in

[4] *Philosophical Review*, XLIX (May, 1940), 361–364.

his *Rationalism and Irrationalism in Religion* (1954), accepted the rationality of the universe, at least in a limited sense, and was not unfriendly to the theistic hypothesis in his effort to construct a scientifically viable and modern rational religious philosophy. The same thing is true of H. J. Paton in his recent *The Modern Predicament* (1955) and of many others, among them writers such as Lloyd Morgan whom Becker otherwise quoted with approval. The case of Lloyd Morgan's *Interpretation of Nature* (1905) is instructive. Beginning with a conception of emergent evolution not so very different from that of the philosopher Alexander, he ends by positing beyond that process, as its ground, an eternal Deity. He does this, not because he believes that the existence of God can be directly proved, but because he considers that thus, and only thus, can the universe be viewed as rational. If this is an act of faith, Morgan would probably reply that it is at least an act of rational faith.

Nor is Becker's contention that the Philosophers, like St. Thomas, accepted their ethical values on faith entirely admissable, for once they had embarked on the road of ethical naturalism the breach with traditional Christian ethics was made, as Theodor Steinbüchel in his brilliant *Zerfall des Christlichen Ethos im XIX Jahrhundert* (1951) has abundantly shown. The fact that St. Thomas concedes to human reason at least as much as F. H. Bradley does in his *Appearance and Reality* (1908) is still no valid reason for absorbing Bradley into the Thomist tradition. Nor does Bradley, after subjecting every concept in terms of which a philosopher might attempt to conceive ultimate reality to the most corrosive criticism, end, like Becker, as a skeptic. His conclusion is rather that the human mind, because of the incurably relational character of thought, is unable to think of the absolute as it is in itself, but that in the absolute all contradictions are somehow eliminated and that reality constitutes a self-consistent, although unintelligible, whole. This position is not so very different from that of St. Thomas.

Surely, Becker was not really serious about beginning an entirely new period in the history of thought with scientific naturalism, and, if he was, this proposal has not been generally accepted, the less so since scientific naturalism, as he well knew, was not absent from eighteenth-century thought. But who can deny that it is this that leads Becker to minimize the negations of the Philosophers and to make the most of their borrowed affirmations?

For the rest, the central argument of the book is stated with Becker's characteristic pungency and clarity. It is this, that the Philosophers substituted for the faith in orthodox Christianity a faith in nature and in the principles of morality; they dismantled the Thomist Heavenly City only to rebuild it again for the habitation, not of the resurrected faithful in another world, but of a wiser and more fortunate humanity that accepts life at the end of life. Hence their ideal of Christian service, their faith in progress and perfectibility, their appeal to posterity, and their religion of humanity. Becker here states in substance what he said in 1943 when he stated that "the values we cherish are the same as those which Jefferson proclaimed and the same as those which for more than 2,000 years the saints and the sages of the world have regarded as the ideal aim and ultimate test of civilized living." [5]

Stated in this way, there is nothing either surprising or startlingly original about Becker's demonstration, though he was certainly right in not finding it emphasized in most of the current literature on intellectual history. Whether you speak of *The Heavenly City* or secularized Christian values makes little difference—the contention itself was an old one. The values of the eighteenth century, its belief in the unity of humanity, in the rights of man, its respect for the human personality, for freedom and equality, were just as axiomatic in the tradition of Christian thought as they are in our own secular society. No student of Western thought will deny today that John Locke and the formulators of the natural rights theory still worked within the medieval and Stoic tradition in ethics and social philosophy. They were still serenely confident of the existence of "natural laws" or fundamental ethical principles and their derivatives, "natural rights," which were inscribed in the human intellect with the same clarity as the laws of logic and mathematics. This had already been a familiar theme in Ernst Troeltsch's *Social Teachings of the Christian Churches* (1923), though some may feel that Becker made an even better case for the argument than did Troeltsch. Again, this same Troeltsch, in his *Der Historismus und seine Probleme* of 1922 had emphasized the same remarkable continuity of Stoic and Christian values in the secularized natural rights theory of the Enlightenment, which he

[5] This is a recurrent theme in Becker's later writing. For a similar statement see his *New Liberties for Old* (New Haven, 1941), 149 f.

found still dominating Western thought insofar as Darwinism had not dislodged it.

Apart from the points already mentioned, the attempt at a critical appraisal of Becker's *The Heavenly City* within the framework of the historical literature on the Enlightenment is confronted with the peculiar dilemma either of accepting his assumptions and then of abstaining from criticism altogether or of criticizing him for the book he did not write and did not intend to write. When Becker chose his title and selected his theme, he was fully aware of the limitations that both imposed, and, being the great writer he was, he was determined to adhere to these limitations whatever the cost.

Once saddled with his title, Becker looks at the Enlightenment as one looks at certain statues, always from a single angle; and, if the analysis is incomplete, he is in a position to reply to the critic that, since he is not writing a history of the Enlightenment, his central themes do not require him to complete it. Many readers must have had a similar experience in perusing his slightly perverse and acidulous chapter entitled "History," a subject which, elsewhere, he plumbed with a depth and perception revealed by no other American historian of his day. What Becker has to say on this subject in *The Heavenly City* is really unexceptionable, although most readers would add that it is patently incomplete. Place this lecture beside the argument of Friedrich Meinecke's *Die Entstehung des Historismus,* published in 1936, and it is difficult to escape the conclusion that Becker's analysis ends where Meinecke's begins, notwithstanding the essential validity of Becker's argument so far as it goes. No one at this time of day will seriously quarrel with

Becker's statement that the historical judgments of the Philosophers were no less tendentious than those of the Christian tradition they were attacking and that they responded to the shock of contact with other cultures and other ages by simply absorbing them into their own habitual categories.

The core problem of eighteenth-century historiography, however, as Meinecke clearly sees, lies elsewhere, lies in penetrating and breaking through the dense wall of the current version of the natural rights philosophy, with its insistence on the stability of human nature in all ages, on its timeless human reason, and on its universally valid truths, and in advancing from the generalizing and typological approach dictated by this philosophy toward a more individualizing, relativistic, and genuinely historical approach to the problem of human evolution. Meinecke, like Becker elsewhere, finds the essential earmarks of thinking in terms of the historical dimension in the twin concepts of individuality (or uniqueness) and development or the march of events, and, while he readily admits that the full triumph of historical thinking was an achievement of the nineteenth century, he contends that its roots were deeply embedded in the eighteenth century, at least in embryonic form.

It is apparent from his discussion of Montesquieu that Becker was thoroughly aware of this problem; yet it seems that his general theme forced him to dwell by preference on the visual blinkers and shortcomings of eighteenth-century historians, to quote repeatedly Hume's remark to the effect that the chief use of history is to "discover the constant and universal principles of human nature," and to devote entire pages to reducing the inflated reputation of Montesquieu to the proper size. All this, says Meinecke, is very true. It is also true that Montesquieu never completely emancipated himself from the natural rights theory, from its crudely schematizing psychology, or from his mechanistic doctrine of causation. Yet Meinecke finds in Montesquieu a plainly perceptible feel for what is individual and unique in the "spirit" of peoples, in their institutions, and in the successive stages of history. Above all he finds in Montesquieu's account of the origins of seigneurial justice in Books 30 and 31 the first genuinely historical and evolutionary analysis of feudalism. Becker, whose thorough grasp of the Philosophers is generally beyond challenge, saw this also but felt that in comparison with the rest of *The Spirit of the Laws* it scarcely weighed in the balance. It is fair to say that the burden of opinion among modern scholars is rather in agreement with Franz Neumann's searching essay in which he contends that Montesquieu is one of the originators of historical thinking and that Meinecke has the better of the argument.[6]

Again, for Meinecke even Hume was one of the trail blazers for the concept of an evolutionary history of the human intellect from barbarism to civilization, for when in his *The Natural History of Religion* (not in his justly more famous *Dialogues*) Hume states that it is only by stages that mankind advances from lower to higher levels of civilization, he was admitting, indirectly at least, that reason, too, has a history. All this is mentioned here merely to raise the question, Was Carl Becker so much the prisoner of the limitations he imposed upon himself

[6] Franz Neumann, Introduction to Montesquieu's *The Spirit of the Laws* (New York, 1949), p. xxxv.

when he chose his arresting but unhappy title of *The Heavenly City* that he was debarred from doing something like justice to this aspect of the Enlightenment? Admittedly, to put the question in this way is to answer it.

It may appear to be both gratuitous and absurd to apply the same critical yardsticks to Becker's lively lectures and Ernst Cassirer's serious historical study of *The Philosophy of the Enlightenment*. Published in the same year 1932, both books have at least this in common that they depart from the traditional practice of taking up the Philosophers individually. Both books fix their attention on fundamental concepts, although the two authors disagree radically on the nature of these fundamental concepts. Cassirer, like Troeltsch, the historian of religion who had spent so much of his life writing about the same continuities which Becker proposed to demonstrate, pointed out the drastic change which the Enlightenment introduced in the whole cosmology of Christian Europe, in the secularization of the Christian ethic that accompanied the belief in the immanence of God in nature, in the jettisoning of the doctrine of original sin and with it the dogma of grace, on which in fact the whole of Christianity rested. Basically, Cassirer agreed also with Steinbüchel's searching study, referred to above, which emphasized the fact that the Philosophers by dispensing with the Christian mystery of the universe also abandoned the traditional Christian humility in the face of that mystery. To be sure, Cassirer was punctiliously careful to point out the permanent and enduring elements in eighteenth-century thought, but in his judgment what was most important in the Enlightenment was tantamount to a radical breach.

Cassirer was certainly no less critical than Becker, but he took hold of the movement at its core, its theory of knowledge, and contended that the methodology of the Philosophers *at its best* and in spite of occasional relapses was neither medieval, nor scholastic, nor mathematical like that of seventeenth-century philosophers, but based rather on a genuinely empirical analysis as described in Newton's *Optics* whether they derived it from Newton or from some other source. Hence Cassirer examined not merely their doctrinal substance, where Becker tended to linger, but pursued their steady or unsteady progression from the older Cartesian rationalism toward an empirical and analytical procedure in the acquisition of truth, which, being now empirically verifiable, had sloughed off the finality and absoluteness of Christian dogma. Cassirer once more placed the emphasis on what Becker tended to minimize, on their struggle for the autonomy of natural and social science and ethics and the emancipation of these disciplines from the thralldom of Christian theology. In this context the "brave youthful blasphemies," Becker's way of describing their radical negation of supernaturalism, became once more a sharp caesura.

By carrying through this demonstration of the progressive abandonment of the a priori or metaphysical foundation of the natural rights theory, by showing that they based their systems of morality and inalienable rights on a naturalistic ethics, on basic human needs and experience, Cassirer placed his finger on the weak link in Becker's argument. What Becker variously calls their retreat from reason or even the bankruptcy of reason was really an abandonment of a one-sided and exclusive

Cartesian rationalism in favor of the empirical method of Locke, Newton, and Hume. It is first with the full acceptance of this approach that the Enlightenment, in Cassirer's view, hits its stride.

In view of Becker's deep and abiding concern with the entire general subject of science and democracy, it is, to say the least, surprising that in *The Heavenly City* he scarcely touches upon one of the really central and pivotal aspects of the Enlightenment—its social science. Except for a brief passage, Cassirer practically ignores it also, and it is especially René Hubert and, more recently, Isaiah Berlin in his *Historical Inevitability* (1954) and elsewhere who once more have called our attention to its central importance. If Becker was bent on exposing the Heavenly City of the Philosophers, here was a heaven-sent opportunity. What I mean is the determined refusal of the Philosophers to draw any distinction between man and nature, between natural and social science, and their confident belief that the rational scheme on which Newton constructed his physical universe and with which Locke, Newton, Hume, and Condillac seemed to be in a fair way to explaining the inner world of thought and emotion, could be applied to state and society also. They cherished a deep conviction that once the laws governing human behavior had been discovered and embodied in a social science or social physics, men's needs could be investigated and satisfied by the most efficient means compatible with psychological and physical facts. They were not yet obsessed by the demon of quantification, but because of this scientific approach they were convinced that the ideal of establishing a wholly just, wholly virtuous, and wholly satisfactory so-

ciety was no longer a utopian dream. Condorcet, whose
Esquisse is the most inspired expression of this belief,
has no doubt that happiness, scientific knowledge, virtue,
and liberty are all bound together "by an indissoluble
chain," while on the other hand stupidity, wickedness,
injustice, and misery are forms of a disease which the
advance of science will eliminate forever.

It would have been easy, as its enemies have consistently done, to deride this optimistic effort of the Enlightenment to construct a social science to support its
faith in reason and nature. It is significant that Carl
Becker did not deride it, though he himself was convinced that such a social science was scarcely feasible.
He did not even believe that the inalienable rights of
man could be shown to be in keeping with the basic
facts of human nature. To him it was a "humane and
genteel faith," no more. On the other hand, he was himself too deeply rooted in the Enlightenment ever to deny
that this age of the Philosophers was one of the most
creditable episodes in the history of mankind.

We conclude by saying that a reflective appraisal of
Becker's *The Heavenly City* that is at once scrupulously
fair and honestly critical remains as difficult today as
when it was first published. It is obviously absurd to
seek in these four stimulating lectures a complete history of the Enlightenment, a task which Becker left to
other more pedestrian historians. They do, however, ex-
hibit a coherent consistency in accord with his basic
assumptions. If what he wanted most to do in this book
was to demonstrate the persistence of cultural values
and behavior patterns through the ages and to show
that the values of traditional democratic ideology were
older and more universal than democracy itself and had

survived in history independently of social systems or even types of civilization, then one can say that Becker wrote "higher history" in Lord Acton's sense of this term. It is not impossible that something like this was in his mind when he wrote the comment on the flyleaf of a friend's copy of the book, "This certainly isn't history. I hope it's philosophy. . . ." [7]

If, however, we take *The Heavenly City* seriously as history, as I think he did and most of us do, then the dilemma mentioned above immediately arises. To the naïve critic who argues that *The Heavenly City* presents neither an adequate nor a well-balanced analysis of the Enlightenment, Becker could reply as Jacob Burckhardt replied to the critics of his *The Civilization of the Renaissance in Italy* that he intended to present only this single view, a view which he and many others thought defensible. To persist in criticizing the book that lies before us, however, exposes us to the risk of saying that Becker did not write the book that we wanted him to write. The book that Becker wanted to write, he actually wrote, indeed, wrote with such superb mastery of form and substance that the ordinary reader involuntarily expects more from it than it can possibly offer. It is not difficult to understand why some scholars, including George Sabine, should regard *The Heavenly City* as Becker's maturest book, though historians as historians might well regret that it should have become his most popular book.[8] With one eye cocked on the literature before and after its pub-

[7] Charlotte W. Smith, *Carl Becker: On History and the Climate of Opinion* (Ithaca, N.Y., 1956), 212.

[8] I refer to the introductory essay by George H. Sabine in Becker, *Freedom and Responsibility* (New York, 1946), which remains the most profound and reflective estimate of Becker that has yet come to my attention.

lication, it is apparent today that the price which Becker paid for the limitations he freely imposed upon himself to write the book he wanted to write was exorbitant, too exorbitant for some of us, for it was not done or, perhaps, could not be done without certain distortions which I have endeavored to point out. Scholarly opinion as to whether these distortions which result from Becker's perspective and emphasis are serious or negligible may vary in accordance with the larger perspective in which we see the Enlightenment.

The position taken here is that in the light of the literature on the eighteenth century that appeared before and after Becker's book these distortions cannot be regarded as being either wholly negligible or unimportant. Nor can this writer, along with many others, persuade himself that in the complex entirety of the Enlightenment the historical continuity of basic Christian values, now secularized, was its most conspicuous feature. The point need not be labored here that the opposite view, that the Enlightenment marks a decisive breach in the Western tradition, is the traditional position of the overwhelming majority of historians of intellectual history. This is not to impugn the validity of applying the principle of continuity to such a historical process as the Enlightenment, but to do so at the expense of its inseparable twin, that of discontinuity, is inevitably to distort. If Burckhardt emphasized the latter at the expense of the former in his *The Italian Renaissance,* Becker reversed the process in his *The Heavenly City.* Both books, despite their brilliance and mastery, are sorely in need of a corrective.

There are, of course, those who are inclined to doubt whether Becker in his inmost thought and apart from the text of *The Heavenly City* seriously intended to challenge what has been called here the traditional view of the Enlightenment. That in his subsequent publications he modified or abandoned some of the positions taken in *The Heavenly City* has already been pointed out. The fact remains, however, that Becker never found it necessary to revise these lectures once they had been published.

PART II

The Reassessment:
Panel Session Commentary

GEOFFREY BRUUN

AUTHOR,

EUROPE AND THE FRENCH IMPERIUM, 1799–1814

4. Carl Becker and the Dignity of Man

SO many eloquent and perceptive tributes have been paid to Carl Becker, as a teacher, writer, and historian, that I fear any comments I can add may seem repetitive. Yet I would like to speak, if I may, of the qualities in his mind and character that impressed me most deeply. He had a singular honesty of thought, a quiet courage, a modesty, gentleness, and humor that all who knew him well remember with affection.

Mr. Becker's prose style, so justly admired for its grace and felicity, its delicate irony, its lightness of touch even when he dealt with difficult subjects, does not convey a just impression of the man himself. In his writing he cultivated an air of detachment, the detachment of a keen observer who stands apart from the human comedy and watches it with quizzical interest. When he analyzed events, when he dissected human acts and motives, he could probe to the heart of an issue with exceptional insight. But he did not give the appearance of being deeply moved himself by the progress of his inquiry, and he seldom betrayed open enthusiasm or indignation at the truths uncovered. To pursue his reflections at leisure and then reduce them to lucid prose seemed to be for him an end in itself. Or such at least was the impression his writing left on many of his admirers.

This detachment, this abstention from dogmatic commitments, displeased more impetuous spirits who hoped to enlist him under their banners. Becker was a tenacious and independent thinker, but he could not see himself as a radical or a proselytizer. "Being a radical," he explained to us once with his self-depreciatory humor, "is a *serious* business."

His diffidence, the gentle irony to which he resorted, the paradoxes he invoked—all these exposed him to misinterpretation. The meaning of his words was usually clear enough because he chose them with scrupulous precision. But the mood was something else, something his readers or listeners had to assess for themselves.

Any attempt to analyze Becker's influence must turn, I suspect, on this question of mood, of intention. It helps to explain the divergent estimates we have heard today about *The Heavenly City of the Eighteenth-Century Philosophers.* Mr. Gottschalk found its prose less satisfactory but its conclusions more valid than he thought them twenty-five years ago. Mr. Gay on the other hand considered it admirably written and scrupulously organized, but he doubted that Becker himself took it "very seriously." *The Heavenly City* was intended, Gay suggested, as "a scintillating collection of aphorisms and paradoxes," and although it has enjoyed a remarkable success Gay regarded its success as "unmerited."

After this preamble, Mr. Gay's decision to analyze *The Heavenly City* "as if Carl Becker had meant every word of it in deadly earnest" might itself appear to squint at paradox. To attack a *jeu d'esprit* in this exacting spirit is to fire cannon balls at cobwebs. Yet many other critics have encountered a similar dilemma when they sought to appraise Becker's writing. How can prose so light and ironical be taken very seriously? How can thoughts so penetrating and often so profound be taken otherwise?

If *The Heavenly City* were no more than a *jeu d'esprit,* we would not be devoting a whole day to a discussion of it on the twenty-fifth anniversary of its presentation. But what is the secret of its effect? To put the question more formally and in broader terms, what was the secret of Becker's influence?

II

Throughout these discussions my thoughts have been turning from the book to Becker himself as I remember him. The year 1931, when he delivered these lectures at the Yale Law School, was the year that he composed his presidential address, "Everyman His Own Historian," for the American Historical Association. It was also the year in which his *Modern History* for secondary-school students was issued. Publishers pursued him with requests for a college text, and he yielded to the extent that he agreed to supervise one. With his chronic digestive ailment depleting his energy and pressed by other commitments, is it not possible that he treated his four

Yale lectures in a casual spirit, regarding them perhaps as a pleasant but irrelevant excursion from more serious tasks?

The answer, it seems to me, must be a definite No. For all their lightness of style, their air of paradox, these Storrs Lectures of 1931 represent a consistent step in Becker's thinking. Their central theme—that "there is more of Christian philosophy in the writings of the *Philosophes* than has yet been dreamed of in our histories"—had received passing reference in his lectures four years earlier, and he phrased the idea in a book review written at the close of 1930.[1] Far from being a playful paradox flung off for the occasion, this theme formed one element of the broader conclusions he was formulating on the need for a new type of historiography, conclusions he continued to amplify throughout the decade that followed.[2]

III

As Mrs. Smith has suggested at one point in her admirable study of Becker, his attitude toward historical facts was reminiscent of Kantian idealism.[3] He also found support for his views in the writings of Schopenhauer and Bergson; but it was perhaps the "As-If" philosophy of Hans Vaihinger that interested him most immediately.[4] The evidence that myths, sincerely entertained, had played a vital part in shaping the beliefs

[1] *Journal of Modern History*, III (March, 1931), 118.

[2] Charlotte Watkins Smith, *Carl Becker* (Ithaca, N.Y., 1956), 211.

[3] *Ibid.*, 53.

[4] *Die Philosophie des Als Op* (Berlin, 1911; 2d ed., 1913); English translation by C. K. Ogden (New York, 1925).

and actions of men in the past invited the conjecture that the postulates considered self-evident today might appear myths to future generations.

Many of Becker's contemporaries felt they had been cast adrift when the attempt to establish a "scientific" history miscarried, when the historical "fact" itself tended to become a disembodied figment of the mind. Becker contributed to its dissolution and was identified as perhaps the most outstanding American proponent of historical relativism. The free play of his thought dismayed some of his colleagues, who charged him with annulling the credentials of his craft without supplying a clue to better ones. Charles A. Beard, in his otherwise favorable review of *The Heavenly City*, complained that it raised profound and pertinent questions but left them unanswered. "Such is the dilemma," Beard concluded, "to which the relativity of the modern historical school inevitably leads." [5]

Becker himself fully recognized the inconclusiveness, the implications of nihilism, in the relativist position. But despite misjudgments to the contrary he was never a sophist. His reading of history persuaded him that more than once adventurous thinking had brought mankind to the brink of an apparently shoreless sea. These dilemmas must be resolved, he felt, not by turning back, but by further courageous speculation—"in the destructive element immerse." Even if there were no certitudes, even if truth was "only the most convenient form of error," [6] it was still important to distinguish, as effectively as one

[5] Charles A. Beard, in *American Historical Review*, XXXVIII (April, 1933), 591.

[6] Carl Becker, *Everyman His Own Historian* (New York, 1935), 245.

could, the more from the less convenient form of myth. How did we, as Becker's students, react to this relativist approach to history? What effects, beneficial or otherwise, do we feel his influence and his example have had upon our thinking? It is obvious, from the diversity of opinions heard at this present session, that he did not train us all to think alike. If called upon to assess his influence, we would doubtless answer each in his own fashion. Yet there is one point on which, I venture to believe, we would all concur—that he did encourage us to think. In pondering how he did so my thoughts have been turning back farther still, to the middle years of the 1920s.

IV

To meet Carl Becker in the flesh was to meet a man unnoteworthy in appearance, unassuming in manner, unemphatic in speech. At my earliest conference with him in the autumn of 1924 the first quality that struck me was his unpretentious simplicity, the second his quiet humor, the third his casual relevance. Gradually, with subsequent sessions, came a feeling of respect so sure and involuntary it took me by surprise. Why, I wondered, did I conceive something close to reverence for this modest and tolerant man, whose wisdom was unobtrusive, whose concern for his students was concealed in casualness, whose sudden chuckles were so homely and unforced.

During the next three years Carl Becker exercised the most powerful influence on my thinking that I have known. But powerful is the wrong word: his influence remained weightless and intangible. There was never the lightest hint of imposition in it. The impulses seemed to arise within me, to take shape as confirmations anticipated rather than received. It seemed to me at times that he gave nothing, neither rules nor advice nor instructions. Yet what he did give was some vital inward reassurance.

Reassurance of what? Here again one encounters the enigma of Becker's influence. He did not provide the positive assistance I had hoped to find—some Ariadne's thread through the academic labyrinth, some shorter passport to the arcana of scholarship. When I suggested that I ought to take a course in methods and bibliography, he said the history department did not offer one. When I asked what works I should read on the French Revolution, he proposed that I browse around the stacks. But wasn't there some particular authority I should study, I insisted, adding that I wanted to improve my French. Well, the library had complete files of the *Intermédiaire des chercheurs et curieux* he volunteered; and suddenly I realized how earnest and stilted I must seem and how gently he was disarming me. He wanted me to discern for myself that graduate study meant more than mastering authoritative texts, that it was an opportunity to enjoy at will the riches of a great library.

Nevertheless, his reluctance to reward my zeal with more precise instructions daunted me. Returning to the White Library, I noted, not for the first time, the Egyptian papyrus framed above the doorway. A fragment from *The Book of the Dead,* I concluded morosely, unaware that its more relevant title is *Book of Going Forth in the Day.* It recalled to my mind the motto of my alma mater, TUUM EST, which we had flippantly translated "It's a tomb," and sometimes more perceptively "It's up to you." Gloomily, while the winter twilight deepened over Lake Cayuga, I wrestled with the thought that perhaps the greatest teachers were those who taught their students how to do without them. Later, when I knew him better, I told Becker with wry amusement how coldly this truth had dawned on me in that hour of uncertainty. He responded with the sudden clearing of his throat that was half a laugh and half a cough. The Cornell system, he conceded, was sometimes described as salutary neglect. He did not know if it was salutary but it might be considered neglect.

It was salutary, but under Becker's guidance it was not neglect. On the morrow of my inconclusive interview I found on my desk a complete set of the mimeographed sheets he prepared for his undergraduate classes. I still have those masterly summations, in which he compressed the essence of each lecture to a few paragraphs followed by a score of relevant titles. Relevant? At the time I debated his concept of relevance. Why, I wondered, did he include *Le crime de Sylvestre Bonnard* on a history list, with the enigmatic comment, "Not a detective story."

In those early days it provoked me that the master I had come three thousand miles to meet did not match my prefiguration of a great scholar. He disclaimed erudition. He appeared, not exactly to disregard, but to be unimpressed by, the emblems and impedimenta of scholarship. His own writings, for all their charm and grace, were neither extensive nor compendious. They revealed no central focus, developed no major theme. His critical reviews excited but disturbed me. Their ironic overtones resembled the luminous play of summer lightning without thunder, as if he found few books serious enough to be taken seriously. His relativist approach to facts and truths and values seemed to involve a suspension of judgment that left one sculpturing in smoke.

These early estimates still survive: I hear them repeated by others when Becker is the subject of critical discussion. But in my own mind a stronger impression long since eclipsed them. It was the conviction that in Carl Becker I had found a man whose patient, unfaltering, independent quest for reality was more intense and single-minded than anything I had known.

It came to me with a growing certainty that the things he deprecated—pretentiousness, affectation, expedients that seduce, prejudices that refract, passions that betray —were impediments to right reason. He did not disown nor undervalue the emotions: he had a sensitive and understanding heart. He did not insist that reason was the sole road to reality for others. But for himself, he was persuaded, the road to reality lay in clear, unfettered thought, and he strove to think clearly with the same unsparing application with which he strove to write clearly.

I came to appreciate too by what calculated labor he made the fruits of his reflection palatable to others. Overearnestness, overintensity, fatigue, were further pitfalls he had taught himself to circumvent on that arduous road. And the detours of circumlocution, the coinages of hollow pedantry, the thralldom of dogmas, the credentials of fallacious authority—how vigilantly he avoided, how democratically he defied them. But the dignity of honest thought in any minds he encountered, critical thinking on any subject, in any age—how instantly his hand went out in greeting, how genuinely he honored such lonely travail.

He was more deeply interested in how people thought

than in what they thought and more concerned to understand them than to judge them, for he was the least censorious of men. The empiricism of Hume, the mystical strain in Pascal, the ambition that transformed Madame Roland, the aspirations that frustrated Henry Adams— all were worthy of meditation because all were clues to the nature of man and to the unique impulse that makes man "play the ape to his dreams." Ideals and aspirations, it seemed to Becker, provided clues the "scientific" historian tended to neglect. "Curiously enough," he observed of Juliette Drouet's idolization of Victor Hugo, "curiously enough this ideal, preposterous in itself no doubt, was in a manner realized; a kind of spiritual regeneration did in fact come to pass, such is the strange power of ideals, even the most unpromising." [7]

V

Becker's insights into history were insights into people, and such consistency as he found in history was the consistency he discerned in human behavior. "When you said that you understood the character you were describing," he asked a seminar student, "did you mean you have thought yourself into him or thought him into yourself?" I recall how eagerly, throughout the remainder of that golden afternoon, we pressed him for answers, until the carillon in the library tower surprised us at a quarter to six. What of the risks of romantic self-deception, we asked, of commencing the quest with an inflated yardstick? What help may novelists and poets and psychologists afford in reading the riddle of man?

[7] *Ibid.*, 260.

Becker and the Dignity of Man

What of mass illusions, of the *Zeitgeist,* of the conjecture that "each age is a dream that is dying, or one that is coming to birth?" How can we achieve objectivity; how can we locate the level of events among so many variables? From what point of reference should the historian start, to what point should he return, to validate his conjectures?

He could start thinking, Becker suggested, with himself, since there was no nearer point at which he could start. Man might not be the measure of all things but he was the measure we were constrained to use. It was not an absolute measure; it could establish no certitudes; it was fallible and inconstant. The biologist and the historian concurred in the opinion that man changes. But there was reason to think that the sum of his propensities, his residual character, had changed less in the course of recorded history than his instruments or his institutions or his art. If this were so, it might be that the soundest norm we could apply, in our efforts to interpret history, was the nature of man himself. We might find that the continuities of history, or such continuities as history appeared to reveal, depended on man's responses to events, and that those responses had more underlying similarity than we were disposed at first thought to expect.

Here, it seems to me, one may discern the positive aspect of Becker's thinking about history, a conception of man implicit throughout his writing. Man's effort to understand the past, no matter how dispassionately, how objectively, it was pursued, remained at bottom an effort to understand himself. "To see in the lessons of history and in the judgments of posterity some standard, more or less absolute, by which the particular act, the concrete institution, might be judged:—what was all this but the effort to discover, as Kant said, 'the constant elements in man's nature in order to understand what sort of perfection it is that best befits him.' " [8]

VI

It has often been pointed out that Becker was a philosopher rather than a historian, and it would be truer still to say that he was an epistemologist. His speculations on the problems of historical evidence, of historical verification, were efforts to ascertain how we know anything at all. To him every man was his own historian because every man must pursue the quest for reality in his own way, must strive, however feebly and fitfully, to orient himself in "his little world of endeavor." [9]

It was in the nature of man that for him there could be no honorable escape from speculation, no legitimate evasion of the imperial quest. He might be no more than "a thinking reed" but his dignity lay in thought, in confronting the mysteries that surrounded him. Because Becker held this faith so honestly, it ennobled the subject of his discourse. To explain his influence by lesser attributes—his lucid analyses, his felicitous prose, his irony or humor or compassion—is to miss the essential secret of that influence. The secret, it seems to me, is simpler and more fundamental. He dignified man.

Dignified and liberated. Everywhere in his writing the heroic and tragic dignity of man is an implicit, a vindicated truth. Everywhere the daunted but indomitable figure of "man thinking" is the recurrent theme. If it

[8] *Ibid.*, 282.   [9] *Ibid.*, 236.

were possible to cite but a single passage to support this view I would choose the moving, the majestic paragraph that closes *Progress and Power*.

You will recall how, on the penultimate page of that unorthodox book, Becker carries the human epic to its present moment in time. He pictures man today, a stranger and afraid, confronting the universe as science represents it. It is a universe not only indifferent to man but unaware of him, oblivious to his existence, his aspirations, and his fate. The concept is one that, three centuries ago, appalled the prescient Pascal: *"Le silence éternal de ces espaces infinis m'effraie."* Yet with a single stroke, a sudden dramatic reversal, Becker reaffirms man's birthright. "The significance of man," he reminds us, "is that he is that part of the universe that asks the question, What is the significance of man?"

Of all that, the universe knows nothing. Apart from man, the universe knows nothing at all—nothing of itself or of infinite spaces, nothing of man or of his frustrated aspirations, nothing of beginnings or endings, of progress or retrogression, of life or death, of good or evil fortune. The cosmic view of the universe of infinite spaces, and of man's ultimate fate within it, is man's achievement—the farthest point yet reached in the progressive expansion of human intelligence and power. It is not rightly to be taken as a description of events that are relevant to man's purposes, but rather as an ideal result of those purposes—the manifestation of his insatiable curiosity, his indefeasible determination to know. As such it is less an objective world of fact than man's creation of the world in his own image. It is in truth man's most ingenious invention, his supreme work of art.

This is Carl Becker on the dignity of man.

WILLSON H. COATES

THE UNIVERSITY OF ROCHESTER

5. Every Word
in Deadly Earnest?

MY remarks can be brief because of my warm endorse-
ment of much that has been said—from the sage introduction by George Sabine, to the implications of the
questions raised by John Hall Stewart, and the comments
which two of my fellow panelists have just made. I was
charmed by Henry Guerlac's recollections from his sensitive adolescence of Carl Becker at ease in intellectual
discourse, and I was enlightened by his compact analysis
of recent research on eighteenth-century science. Peter
Gay's indictment of *The Heavenly City* seemed to me
brilliantly executed, but I agree entirely with Leo Gershoy's critique, which was both magnanimous and penetrating. Similarly, Walter Dorn's detached appraisal of
The Heavenly City found me nodding in approval.[1]

   The Heavenly City is, indeed, a classic of its kind, but
it was never intended to be a fully rounded study of the

[1] Considerably expanded and modified versions of remarks by
Messrs. Stewart and Gershoy are included below, 156–173, 191–
207.

eighteenth-century *philosophes*. The very first paragraph of the book gives clear evidence that these were lectures conceived in Becker's engaging ironic vein. If the book has been taken as if Becker meant every word in deadly earnest and if it has been recommended as a comprehensive exposition of the Enlightenment, that is a reflection not on Becker but on the subtlety of American scholars. On the other hand, Becker did seriously intend to expose a neglected facet of eighteenth-century thinking—the unconscious emotional commitments of an age that has been represented in its preromantic phase as cynical, antireligious, and coldly rational.

The Heavenly City, then, should be read in the context of the historiography of the eighteenth century up to 1931, even as a corrective to Becker's own earlier work on the eighteenth century, especially his *The Declaration of Independence.* Had the lectures been delivered in 1941 instead of 1931, Becker would certainly have adopted a different tone. Nazi totalitarianism at its menacing peak was a secular religion that Becker did not regard so dispassionately as he did the French Revolution, for the very conditions which permitted the detached irony of 1931 were threatened by the Nazis.

I do not wish to imply that, given the circumstances under which Becker's lectures were delivered, he is above criticism. No one I have known was so free from pompous rectitude, and Becker would have enjoyed the scholarly assault we have witnessed today. This should be controverted, however, by the kind of historical-minded evaluation of *The Heavenly City* which Becker himself was wont to give to the classics of the eighteenth century.

Such an estimate would be complex, and among its

87

components would be a recognition that every classic, from the day of its publication, has an intellectual history of its own over which the author has no control. It is, in this connection, quite legitimate for Mr. Gay to point to the exploitation of *The Heavenly City* by the New Conservatives; but he is, I think, wrong in assuming that Becker would "have been appalled at such disciples." It would have been more characteristic of him to say blandly that he was flattered to see his little book put to different uses, as though it were analogous to the reflections of Plato or Aristotle.

Whatever transient comfort *The Heavenly City* may afford those of one persuasion or another, there is no doubt to what tradition of Western thinking the book and Becker himself belong—that of both rationalism and empiricism, which are quite compatible with each other if one is not too literal-minded about their different premises. Becker was, despite the anti-intellectualism logically implicit in some versions of his relativism, one of those modern thinkers who recognized the danger to man's faith in reason, arising from ignorance of the emotions covertly at work in mental processes. He never succumbed to the defeatism of the genuine anti-intellectual. On the contrary, he was confident that the reasoning propensities of his students and his readers were hardy enough to survive the exposure of man's capacity for self-deception. Thus I am inclined to disagree with the observation made by a well-known historian not present at this colloquy, that there is in the beautifully written *Heavenly City* a "corrosive skepticism." This historian, like any worthy scholar, has remained uncorrupted by his reading of it.

Comments by LOUIS GOTTSCHALK

THE UNIVERSITY OF CHICAGO AS SUMMARIZED
BY JOHN HALL STEWART

6. Becker and the
Philosophes' Dilemma

MR. GOTTSCHALK began his remarks by indicating that he agreed with very little that had so far been said on Becker's *The Heavenly City*. Because the purpose of the conference was to reassess that book, he had carefully reread it in recent weeks. He had been less pleased with its style than upon his first reading of it, but on the other hand he was more convinced of the correctness of the book's main thesis, although less impressed with its originality. In all fairness to Becker, the speaker pointed out that his own standards of style were largely derived from Becker and that, if the thesis of *The Heavenly City* twenty-five years after its publication seemed no longer new, part of the reason for its familiarity was that the book itself had helped to make its theme common property.

The Heavenly City, Gottschalk thought, could not fairly or usefully be assessed as an effort to portray the

Enlightenment as a whole or even to summarize all the religious views of the *philosophes*. As the book's title implied and its first chapter plainly indicated, Becker's purpose was merely to inquire how thick was the cake of customary Christian thinking upon the religious thought of the *philosophes*. His answer was: "There is more of Christian philosophy in the writings of the *Philosophes* than has yet been dreamt of in our histories."[1] Although he seems to have given some readers the impression that he considered the Thomists and the *philosophes* otherwise largely similar, he nevertheless made obvious that such was not his intention. Again and again he indicated his awareness of the differences between the two sets of thinkers (see, among others, the passage omitted by Mr. Gay in his quotation from *The Heavenly City*, p. 8). Still, in his eagerness to impress upon his hearers his point of view (let's not forget that these chapters were originally lectures), he naturally stressed the similarities.

What Becker found that was similar in Thomists and *philosophes* was a large element of confidence in reason to solve the ethical problems of mankind smoothly. *The Heavenly City* was not Becker's first essay on the ethics of the *philosophes*. In his "The Dilemma of Diderot" first published around 1915,[2] Becker had raised the question why Diderot never during his own lifetime published *Le neveu de Rameau*, and he came to an answer much like that he gave in *The Heavenly City* not only for Diderot but also for Hume (whose *Dialogues concerning Natural Religion* was also published only posthumously):

[1] *Heavenly City*, 31.
[2] Reprinted in *Everyman His Own Historian* (New York, 1935), 262–283.

both authors were puzzled by the effects their skeptical attitude toward traditional religion might have on the practice of traditional virtue. It makes small difference to the correctness of Becker's main thesis if other reasons can also be found for their restraint in publishing their books or even if his explanation of it in *The Heavenly City* should be totally incorrect, for from other sources he indicates convincingly that concern regarding what happens to standards of virtue in a materialistic world greatly troubled these two eighteenth-century writers.

Becker seems to have held all his life that some problems of mankind (the ethical problem prominent among them) are persistent, and the answers of each age to them sound more different than they actually prove to be upon close examination. An examination of Becker's *The Heavenly City* chapter by chapter, Gottschalk said, would show that Becker's main purpose was to see how the *philosophes* handled the persistent problem of human morality.

Chapter I is entitled "Climates of Opinion." Its purpose is to indicate that different ages use different vocabularies to answer their fundamental questions because their vocabularies are based upon different major premises; where the thirteenth century's major premise was God, the eighteenth's was Reason, and the twentieth's is History and Science. Since the modern mind is historical, Becker claims that he, as a product of the modern world, has to think historically: "Before the historian can do anything with Newton and Voltaire, he has to make it clear that they came, historically speaking, after Dante and Thomas Aquinas and before Einstein and H. G. Wells." [3]

[3] *Heavenly City*, 28.

For all their differences in major premises and therefore in vocabulary, "at every turn the *Philosophes* betray their debt to medieval thought" [4] because "the underlying preconceptions of eighteenth-century thought were still, allowance made for certain important alterations in the bias, essentially the same as those of the thirteenth century." [5]

The second chapter, Gottschalk continued, was entitled "The Laws of Nature and of Nature's God." Here Becker maintained that the eighteenth-century *philosophe* was not so cynical as he appeared on the surface to be. Even Voltaire's epigram, "History is after all only a pack of tricks we play on the dead," was only "a witticism intended to brand dishonest historians." [6] The *philosophe's* vocabulary was no longer built around *God* and it had not yet got to *relativity* and *evolution,* but "no enlightened person could reach a restful conclusion" without *nature, natural law,* and the like.[7] "*The Heavenly City* thus shifted to earthly foundations," [8] and Holy Writ was replaced by "the great book of nature." [9] Design in nature was no longer "a logical construction dwelling in the mind of God" but had "taken on a more familiar and substantial body." [10] Although Becker attributed a large part of this metamorphosis of attitudes to Newton, the validity of Becker's major theme, Gottschalk contended, did not diminish with any demonstration that the eighteenth century was still largely Cartesian (as, indeed, Becker had pointed out anyway on pp. 134–36 and more fully in *The Declaration of Independence*). For Becker's point is that *laws* of *nature* and *reason* (whether

[4] *Ibid.*, 30. [5] *Ibid.*, 31. [6] *Ibid.*, 44. [7] *Ibid.*, 47.
[8] *Ibid.*, 49. [9] *Ibid.*, 51. [10] *Ibid.*, 55.

Cartesian or Newtonian) were, in men's vocabularies, re-placing *laws of God* and *faith*. Notwithstanding their new phrases, the *philosophes* still were faced with "the ugly dilemma, emerging from the beautiful premise of the new philosophy: if nature is good, then there is no evil in the world; if there is evil in the world, then nature is so far not good." [11]

In Chapter III, "The New History: Philosophy Teach-ing by Example," Gottschalk continued, Becker showed that the *philosophes* tried to use the lessons of history as a substitute for Christian morality. They wanted a better society, but "they did not ask how society had come to be what it was, but how it could be made better than it was." [12] Hence they were not detached historians of the now commonly approved fashion. Rather they were pious wishers who subscribed to a set of beliefs that were essentially a religious creed, of which, however, "the articles . . . were at every point opposed to those of the established philosophy" of the Catholic Church:

(1) man is not natively depraved; (2) the end of life is life itself, the good life on earth instead of the beatific life after death; (3) man is capable, guided solely by the light of rea-son and experience, of perfecting the good life on earth; and (4) the first and essential condition of the good life on earth is the freeing of men's minds from the bonds of ignorance and superstition, and their bodies from the arbitrary oppres-sion of the constituted social authorities.[13]

Becker distinguished between the good and the bad historians of the eighteenth century (and he obviously admired the work of the good historians). Yet even the

[11] *Ibid.*, 69.   [12] *Ibid.*, 97.   [13] *Ibid.*, 102–103.

best historians among them, he contended,[14] wrote their history to point the moral that justified their creed: "Mankind has at last emerged, or is emerging, from the dark wilderness of the past into the bright, ordered world of the eighteenth century." [15]

But what of the future? The last chapter, entitled "The Uses of Posterity," Gottschalk went on, gave Becker's analysis of the *philosophes'* answer to that question. "The Philosophers called in posterity to exorcise the double illusion of the Christian paradise and the golden age of antiquity. For the love of God they substituted love of humanity; for the vicarious atonement the perfectibility of man through his own efforts; and for the hope of immortality in another world the hope of living in the memory of future generations." [16] Hence: "The doctrine of progress, of perfectibility [Becker unfortunately did not distinguish between the two words, but the distinction is not necessary for the validity of his major theme], became an essential article of faith in the new religion of humanity." [17] And so: "The thought of posterity was apt to elicit from eighteenth-century Philosophers and revolutionary leaders a highly emotional, an essentially religious response. Posterity, like nature, was often personified, reverently addressed as a divinity, and invoked in the accents of prayer." [18] Using Diderot as representative of the *philosophes,* Becker maintained:

The ideas, the phrases are essentially religious, essentially Christian: for the worship of God, Diderot has substituted respect for posterity; for the hope of immortality in heaven, the hope of living in the memory of future generations. . . .

---

[14] See analysis, *ibid.,* 108–118.   [15] *Ibid.,* 118.
[16] *Ibid.,* 130.   [17] *Ibid.,* 139.   [18] *Ibid.,* 142.

The Philosophes' *Dilemma*

The essence of the matter Diderot managed to reduce to an epigram: "Posterity is for the Philosopher what the other world is for the religious." [19]

Becker's last chapter concludes with an effort to show that the same dilemma—why should man strive for the good if he is mere matter without hope of immortality?—is a problem of the twentieth-century Marxist. Digression though this conclusion may be, it illustrates, said Gottschalk, Becker's conviction that the problems of mankind of all eras are the same, the answers differing only in vocabulary not in essence. The last words of the book are a quotation from Marcus Aurelius: "The man of forty years, if he have a grain of sense, in view of this sameness has seen all that has been and shall be." *Quod erat demonstrandum;* Becker has shown that the eighteenth-century Philosopher's faith in the good ending was more like the thirteenth-century Christian's than most previous historians had perceived. Gottschalk suggested that any who doubted that that was all Becker was trying to do in this particular book and had succeeded in doing it should reread the book and then reread Condorcet's *Tableau des progrès de l'esprit humain.*

[19] *Ibid.,* 149–150.

BEATRICE F. HYSLOP

HUNTER COLLEGE

7. From Manuscript to Print: Some Reflections and Comments

CRITICS and defenders of Carl Becker's *The Heavenly City of the Eighteenth-Century Philosophers* agree that Carl Becker was a great teacher. His lack of oratorical flair and his reserve established a plane of intellectualism less appreciated by the average layman than by the initiated, especially the better students in his seminars. Like the *philosophes,* who were optimistic of man's capacity to apprehend truth if untrammeled reason was pursued and nature given free reign, Becker taught in the true eighteenth-century spirit. His aim was always to stimulate thought, even if divergent from his own, rather than to impose ideas or dispense specific historical fact. Carl Becker's name deserves to be placed in a historical Hall of Fame of great teachers, along with such of his contemporaries as James Harvey Robinson, Charles A. Beard, and Carlton J. H. Hayes.[1] All of these also taught outside the classroom by lecture and by the printed word. Would Socrates have achieved fame had he not taught Plato and a small circle of choice spirits? Becker and Becker's reputation live on through the teaching of his best students as well as through his writings.

The Heavenly City conveyed the impact of his intellect to a very wide public, to the audience he addressed in person and to all readers of the published lectures. Without knowledge of the actual composition and size of the audience that heard the original lectures at Yale in April, 1931, nor of the immediate response,[2] one is safe in concluding that Becker's novel reflections have been disseminated over the years largely through the published version now in its tenth printing. Although *The Heavenly City* has had a noteworthy popularity in the United States, it has never been translated into French and is probably not widely known in Europe, even among specialists on the eighteenth century. Perhaps it is the American historians of American thought, already schooled in Becker's two classics—on the American Revolution and on the Declaration of Independence [3]—who

---

[1] The author of this article was never a student of Becker's but she wrote her doctoral thesis under Carlton J. H. Hayes. Although she had one or two contacts with Carl Becker, her chief knowledge of him has been through his writings. She used his high-school textbook in modern history during two years of teaching at the Kingswood School for Girls, Bloomfield Hills, Michigan.

[2] Correspondence with Yale University brought only negative replies. Time did not permit an effort to discover references to the lectures in Becker's correspondence.

[3] *The Eve of the Revolution* (New York, 1921) and *The Declaration of Independence* (New York, 1922).

have looked upon *The Heavenly City* as an authoritative history of European philosophy and given the little volume an exalted importance that it does not deserve in the whole historiography of the eighteenth century. The absence, however, of any outstanding, short treatment of eighteenth-century thought has contributed to the success of Becker's printed lectures.[4]

Examination of Becker's original typed manuscript, with handwritten excisions and corrections, preserved in the Cornell Library and kindly made available to this author through a microfilmed copy, throws light on the composition of the lectures and on the changes ultimately incorporated in the published volume.[5] Charlotte Watkins Smith has already demonstrated, in her revealing

[4] Daniel Mornet's classic (*Les origines intellectuelles de la Révolution française, 1715–1787* [Paris, 1933]), has never been translated, but both his book and Kingsley Martin's volume (*French Liberal Thought in the Eighteenth Century* [Boston, 1929]), are more than two to four times as long as Becker's work. The chapter on the eighteenth century in Crane Brinton's *Ideas and Men* (New York, 1950) is excellent but should not be isolated from the discussion of centuries before and after.

[5] The author's teaching schedule did not permit a visit to the Cornell library for comparison of the original typed manuscript and the published volume when this article was first solicited. She wishes to express special gratitude to Miss Gussie E. Gaskill, librarian of the President White Historical Library at Cornell University, and to Mr. Phil L. Snyder, formerly assistant archivist at Cornell, for providing her with the microfilm of the typed manuscript of *The Heavenly City*. Pages of the typed copy are usually numbered consecutively by chapter. All page references are to the printed book unless indicated. The typed original will be referred to as the manuscript. Thanks are also due to Professor Rockwood as editor.

chapter devoted to Becker's "Practice of Writing," the great care he took in composition.[6] Becker usually started with a handwritten draft and then made successive typed copies until he was satisfied with the content and its expression. Unfortunately, a first handwritten manuscript of *The Heavenly City* has not been preserved. The typed copy studied for this paper required 210 frames of microfilm; yet it is incomplete, since it stops with page 153 of the printed text. The Cornell Library has another typed copy—the final one used by the printer.

Differences between the original typed text and the printed book fall into four categories. First, there are minor changes of single words or phrases, such as the substitution of "carefully" for "meticulously" on the fifth line of page 6 of the book. Secondly, passages are crossed out on the typed text but nevertheless appear in the printed text. The reproduction of page 58 of the book (typed page 36) included here illustrates this category and also Becker's own handwritten insertions. This page demonstrates the relative unimportance of many of the revisions. The third category, involving references that are transposed from one spot in the manuscript to another in the book, is shown by Becker's use of Voltaire's oftquoted statement, "History is after all only a pack of tricks we play on the dead." Whereas the typed version of page 36 in the book carries the quotation, Becker dropped it from that position before the book was printed. The two versions of page 36 may be compared:

[6] *Carl Becker* (Ithaca, N.Y., 1956), chap. v. Chapter IV is entitled "The Art of Writing." The only references of *The Heavenly City* are on pages 123, 140, 165, 192 ff., 211–212.

as occult ~~forces~~ qualities, supposed to result from the specific
forms of things, but as genuine laws of nature, by which the
things themselves are formed." (Optics). Thus was the ~~essence~~
~~of the new and true philosophy~~ *new way to knowledge seus of by* Natural Philosophy: to "search
into the things themselves", and then to formulate the "genuine
~~laws of nature , by which the things themselves are formed."~~

Certainly this new philosophy ravished the eighteenth
century into admiration; and not the least astonishing thing
about it was the common place methods employed to discover
such marvelous truths. That Newton discovered the nature of
light *seemed even less significant to his contemporaries* ~~was even less astonishing~~ than that he did so by playing
with a prism. It was as if nature had for the first time
been brought close to men, close enough to be tangible, and
clearly visible in all its wonderful details. Nature, it seemed,
was after all just the common things that common men observed and
handled every day, and natural law only the uniform way these
things behaved. Steam bubbling from the spout of a kettle,
smoke whisking up a chimney, morning mist *lifting* ~~rising~~ from meadows --
here was nature all about, moving in ways not mysterious her
wonders to perform; and revealing, to the eyes of common men, no
less than to the learned, those laws that imposed on all things
their ~~curious and intricate~~ reasonable and beneficent, even if
curious and intricate, commands.

When philosophy became a matter of handling testtubes instead
of dialectics every one could be, in the measure of his
intelligence and interest, a philosopher. ~~About It was about~~
~~1748 that Franklin began to play with the "electric tube"~~
~~that Peter Collinson sent to the Philadelphia Library. "I never~~

Reproduction of page 36 of Chapter II of the typed manuscript, page 58 of
the printed text. (Courtesy of the Cornell University Archives.)

From Manuscript to Print

Typed Manuscript	*Printed Version*
It is true . . . as everyone knows. And how neat and irresistible it is— "History is after all a pack of tricks we play on the dead."—"If God did not exist it would be necessary to invent him."—"Nothing is more annoying than to be obscurely hanged." The list would be long. . . . But the wit is too superficially cynical [MS p. 6].	It is true you will find plenty of cynical wit—in Voltaire above all, as everyone knows. But the wit is too superficially cynical to be more than a counterirritant.

In the book, both the "pack of tricks" and the "obscurely hanged" quotations are transferred to pages 43–44, where they support Becker's reiteration of the point already made on page 36 regarding the superficial cynicism of eighteenth-century negations. The "pack of tricks" quotation bolsters Becker's thesis that moderns tend to read more into Voltaire's statements than he probably intended; the same citation does double duty by re-emerging on page 88, this time to reinforce Becker's own modern interpretation of eighteenth-century history.

The most significant type of revision made by Becker—the fourth category—concerns passages in the manuscript which have been omitted completely from the book. Among numerous other examples only those most worthy of notice will be identified. The change in the wording of the dedication, for instance, reveals the delicacy of Becker's thought.

Typed Manuscript	*Printed Version*
To Frederick Jackson Turner and Charles Homer Haskins who	To Charles Homer Haskins and Frederick Jack-

Typed Manuscript (cont.)	*Printed Version* (cont.)
for forty years have been my teachers, and to whom I owe more than can be expressed in words, this book is dedicated.	son Turner, His Friends and Teachers, The Author Dedicates This Book In Gratitude and Affection.

The date of the printed preface is May, 1932. Turner died in March, 1932, but Haskins lived until 1937, by which time the volume had already established a reputation. Phrased more precisely and gracefully, the second dedication expresses a more personal touch.

Insight into Becker's purpose in presenting the lectures is revealed by two widely separated statements present in the manuscript but omitted from the book. The first comes at the very end of the first chapter ("Climates of Opinion") immediately following the succinct last lines of the printed text:

In spite of all of it, there is more of Christian philosophy in the writings of the *Philosophes* than has yet been dreamt of in our histories.

In the following lectures I shall endeavor to elaborate this theme. I shall attempt to show that the underlying preconceptions of eighteenth-century thought were still, allowance made for certain important alterations in the bias, essentially the same as those of the thirteenth century. I shall attempt to show that the *Philosophes* demolished the Heavenly City of St. Augustine only to rebuild it with more up-to-date materials [p. 31].

The original typed text continued:

It is my thesis. [Then beginning again.] In short, my thesis (if you will allow . . . an objective historian to have a thesis, provided he does not aggressively defend it) is that the eighteenth century world pattern was a mediaeval design done in modern colors, its climate of opinion no more than a springtime amelioration of the mediaeval winter, with whatever obvious indications, in the prevailing breezes, of sultry heat to come [no page no.].

This passage is of particular significance because it shows clearly the tentative and cautious nature of the interpretation Becker proposed to defend in *The Heavenly City.* While the reference to "objective historians" might on the surface appear as a shaft directed at the "new historians," it is more clearly a subtle dig by a "new historian" at the old. This reference and the imaginative and colorful analogy to painting were probably omitted as irrelevant asides that added little to the effectiveness of a case already adequately presented. Becker chose concise language and achieved a greater impact.

Another section defining his objectives which Becker dropped would have appeared in the last chapter ("The Uses of Posterity") on p. 123 of the book:

Typed Manuscript	*Printed Version*
. . . never collide. The purpose of these lectures is to exhibit the common ground on which the philosophers met the enemy and in some measure defeated Christian Philosophy. The rational character of the universe (as I endeavored to show in the second lecture) was . . . a preconception common to mediaeval and eighteenth century thought;	. . . ideas that rush toward each other on different levels of apprehension will pass without conflict or mutual injury because they never establish contact, never collide. In order to defeat Christian philosophy the Philosophers had therefore to meet it on

Beatrice F. Hyslop

but whereas the theologians deduced the rational universe from the character of God as revealed in holy writ and proclaimed on the authority of the Church, the philosophers inferred the character of God from the rational nature of the universe as revealed by observation and proclaimed on the authority of Reason. Another common preconception (and it is with this that we are most concerned) was that the history of the world is a dramatic exemplification of . . . [no page no.].

the level of certain common preconceptions.

A break in the typed text occurred here.

The explicit statement of purpose, ultimately left out, added little that had not been said implicitly throughout the lectures. The whole omitted passage may have been designed to brief those of the audience who had missed the earlier talks, although it is not clear whether the material was in fact included in the lecture as actually delivered. Having ventured into what must have appeared, on reflection, to be a digression, Becker evidently decided to omit the whole passage in favor of greater emphasis upon the underlying confidence in the significance of the human drama shared by both the medieval and the eighteenth-century minds.

Inadvertently, by eliminating the colorful passage in the first case, Becker tended to strengthen an appeal to the reason of his listeners, whereas the dropping of the second, an analysis of the rationality of the two centuries, had the consequence of making a more imaginative appeal. This apparently contradictory effect was undoubtedly the result of a conscious effort to avoid digressions and to increase the clarity of the argument. Had Becker included the two omissions, they would have further demonstrated his sincerity of purpose and have provided an answer to Professor Gay's suggestion, at the beginning of his paper, that Becker may not have taken the lectures seriously, that they were a *"jeu d'esprit,* a collection of aphorisms and paradoxes meant to stimulate and (I suspect) to shock his audience." [7]

Yet another omission occurs in the early pages of the famous first chapter, where, making use of Whitehead's phrase, Becker presents his classic analysis of the climate of opinion. This concept was already implicit in Becker's own thought, and through this chapter he carried it to a wide sector of contemporary thought. Dante and St. Thomas are, for instance, brought to life in the passage in the original manuscript, omitted from page 2 of the printed text, where Becker refers to the differing personal climates to be found in the same age as well as the widely divergent preconceptions of two different ages. In these omitted lines, Becker notes the tendency of

---

[7] Mr. Gay modified slightly the text read at Colgate before its publication in the *Political Science Quarterly,* LXXII (June, 1957), pp. 182–199. Although a few sharp implications were omitted at the beginning, the tone of the article remains very critical of Becker's *The Heavenly City.* The phrase quoted here was retained in the printed text (p. 182), although the more pointed statement as to Becker not taking his lectures seriously was omitted.

thinkers to accept and not to challenge fundamental ideas held in common. When the eighteenth century retained ideas of Christian philosophy, it did not debate them. The *philosophes* were far more concerned, according to Becker, with the exposition and defense of their new interpretations than with the justification of earlier Christian ideas.

When Becker delivered his lectures, Americans were passing through the depression. His veiled jibes at the naïve optimism of the eighteenth century were destined to strike a responsive chord in the minds of listeners and readers worried about the whole structure of contemporary society. His audience must have included many law students, and lawyers were then more concerned with substantive law than with such abstractions as the relation of law to universal laws of nature. Far more secular-minded than the eighteenth century, the early-1930 generation was undoubtedly thinking less of the Christian climate of opinion still surviving than of pragmatic considerations. Becker's thesis that eighteenth-century philosophy held more in common with the great Christian era of the thirteenth century than was usually believed was an unorthodox interpretation in 1931 well calculated to appeal to those affected by the depression. Becker was inserting, in an age of skepticism and disillusionment, something new into the analyses of eighteenth-century thought, a philosophy so basic to American ideals and institutions.

Thus, appraisal of *The Heavenly City* should not be isolated from the climate of opinion of the 1930s, nor should one lecture be taken by itself since all four are carefully integrated by references backward and forward.

A single chapter might cause the reader to re-examine his own thinking but would leave him with a fragmentary and sometimes incomprehensible picture of the over-all historical implications of the book. The first chapter on the climate of opinion has been more widely used than the others. Becker was not, however, merely aiming to challenge individual thinking but was discussing a historical thesis. Lack of significant appraisal of this thesis until the colloquium at Colgate twenty-five years after it was presented resulted from the climate of opinion of the 1930s and from the use of parts of *The Heavenly City* out of context or without reference to the whole.

Let us accept Becker's avowed and tacit purpose and explore further the implications for his thought of other passages presented in the manuscript but omitted from the published text. Throughout the book and not merely in single chapters, Becker deals with religion, the idea of progress, and the nature of history. Mr. Gay, in his oral criticism of *The Heavenly City* implied that Becker misunderstood Christianity and therefore saw a false continuity between Christian values of the Middle Ages and the views of the *philosophes*.[8] The religious ideas held by Becker and his critics naturally play a part in such criticism. Becker was a relativist in religion as well as in history. Statements that bear on Becker's understanding of Christianity and that underlie his interpretation, appear not only in the second chapter, "The Laws of Nature and of Nature's God," but in many places in his four lectures. This dispersal is confusing to the reader but was undoubtedly the consequence of Becker's effort to reach

[8] Refers to informal remarks by Mr. Gay at the afternoon session.

an audience that shifted partially each day. A few
changes in the text, some passages crossed out of the
original yet retained in the printed text, and some not
appearing in the printed volume suggest significant refinements of Becker's thinking.

In the first chapter, after the verse on page 10 of the
printed version where Becker has been discussing Dante's
philosophical method, a fairly long paragraph in the
typed manuscript explained in more detail Dante's four
ways of analyzing the meaning of a text: the literal, the
allegorical, the moral, and the anagogical ("above the
sense"). Then followed:

Thus it was possible by means of a highly intricate dialectic,
supported on occasion by symbolism, to justify the ways of
God to man. [The next passage was written in Becker's own
handwriting.] If this method of squaring reason seems fantastic to us, it is only because we employ other methods. To
St. Thomas it would no doubt have seemed fantastic to employ
the method of modern science [MS p. 15; illegible passages
follow].

Becker was not arguing the modernity of St. Thomas
and Dante, as do the neo-Thomists of the present day;
rather, he was alleging the Christian substrata of
eighteenth-century thought. This omitted passage also
illustrates the infinite care Becker took with the literary
quality of the finished text.

Remarks about Voltaire as a "man of faith" are an important part of Becker's argument on the relationship of
the thirteenth and eighteenth centuries. Note the difference between the typed and printed texts of page 8,
line 12.

108

From Manuscript to Print

Typed Manuscript	Printed Version
But this use of the word [rationalist] is unfortunate, since it serves to obscure the fact that Voltaire was a man of faith, although not of faith in Christian doctrine, and the [*sic*] St. Thomas employed reason to defend the very doctrine that Voltaire denied [MS p. 12].	But this use of the word is unfortunate, since it obscures the fact that reason may be employed to support faith as well as to destroy it.

On the typed original the words beginning "Voltaire was a man of faith . . ." were crossed out, and the phrase used in the printed text, "reason may be employed . . . ," was inserted by hand. On page 36, following the sentence, "There is more fundamental pessimism to be found in the seventeenth than in the eighteenth century, in the *Libertins* than in the *Philosophes*," appeared the following lines, crossed out in the typed text, and omitted from the printed text:

Even Voltaire, who almost single-handed gave his century its reputation for cynicism, was no La Bruyère; one might say that Voltaire above all is no La Bruyere [MS p. 6 of chap. ii].

The two passages omitted from the printed text of *The Heavenly City* reinforce other statements depicting Voltaire as a man of faith and a reformer and not merely a destructive cynic and demonstrate Becker's genuine penetration into the subtleties of the eighteenth-century mind. Norman L. Torrey did not publish his *The Spirit of Voltaire* until 1938, in which he confirmed Becker's thesis by establishing the positive side of Voltaire's thought, little noted by earlier historians of eighteenth-century thought. Had Becker included these two passages and used Voltaire's witticism on the nature of history differently, would the argument of the final sentence of the first printed paragraph on page 37 have been bolstered and, to some ears, have sounded less facetious and more sincere?

Voltaire, skeptic—strange misconception! On the contrary, a man of faith, an apostle who fought the good fight, tireless to the end, writing seventy volumes to convey the truth that was to make us free.

Or is one forced to conclude that, in both these omissions, Becker's literary judgment was sound? In the final version, has he not succeeded in making his point clearly and precisely? Would the omitted material really have added anything vital to his thesis?

Becker also chose to let Voltaire define natural religion for him: "Let Voltaire define natural religion: 'I understand by natural religion the principles of morality common to the human race.' " [9] Yet Becker recognized that Voltaire and the *philosophes* derived morality and virtue from Christian philosophy.

The position that Becker assigned to atheism in eighteenth-century thought is also a significant feature of his discussion of religion. The fact that Hume did not publish his atheistical *Dialogues* when he wrote them— a fact often overlooked by philosophers—is an important link in Becker's argument. They were not published until 1779, after Hume's death. The force of this argument at the end of the chapter on Nature's God is strengthened by Becker's use of this delay in publication again in

[9] *Heavenly City*, 44.

the beginning of the next chapter on history. Becker's thesis suggests that the *philosophes*, like Hume, unable to rationalize their faith before 1750, turned thereafter to history for justification. Although Hume's thought was undoubtedly known to his friends, the book appeared after thinkers had already turned from philosophic speculation to practical reform programs. Thus, to Becker, the atheistic Baron d'Holbach, La Mettrie, and some others are isolated individuals rather than types characteristic of the majority of *philosophes*.

Becker distinguishes between deism and atheism in eighteenth-century thought. Belief in Nature's God is not, for him, atheistic, even when deism rejected certain aspects of traditional Christianity. A passage omitted from page 76 of the book suggesting that the *philosophes* also drew back from atheistical implications of Cartesian logic, and that atheists "were only following the Goddess of Reason," appeared in print as: "Yet the atheists were only following the Goddess of all the Philosophers. . . ." By the omissions Becker avoided confusion between reason as an ideal of philosophy and the Parisian ceremony to the Goddess of Reason held late in 1793. Becker denies that this atheistical effort of a few *enragés* during three or four months (1793–1794) was typical of the French Revolution. He claims the ideals of Liberty, Equality, and Fraternity, and the public fêtes designed by David to dramatize these ideals, were basically religious, although anti-Catholic, and illustrates the influence of the deism of the *philosophes* in his treatment of Robespierre's worship of the Supreme Being. Becker belittles both the qualitative and quantitative importance of atheism in the thought of the eighteenth century and thereby indirectly

111

strengthens his argument for the debt of the *philosophes* to Christianity.

Changes in the religious climate of opinion since the 1930s inevitably play a role in reinterpretation of *The Heavenly City* in the 1950s. In the 1930s, liberal Christianity was gaining ascendance after attacks by the higher criticism on literalism and creeds. Deism was generally accepted as a naturalist phase of Christianity, harmonious with modern science. Today, however, after the neo-paganism of Nazism, the avowed atheism of communism, and the postwar growth of neo-orthodoxy and of fundamentalism, there has been a tendency to look upon deism as unchristian and synonymous with atheism. The gulf between a theist and a Humanist approach to religion is deeper today than it was in the 1930s. Theist readers of *The Heavenly City* today would deny validity to Becker's ascription of Christian influences in the religion of most of the *philosophes* of the eighteenth century and label all naturalism atheistic. On the other hand, Humanists ignore the publication date of Hume's *Dialogues* in assessing atheistical influence in the eighteenth century and thereby overemphasize the *philosophes* as atheistical forerunners of modern Humanism. The reader's own religious views are an important key to the appraisal of Becker and his *The Heavenly City.*

Although the third lecture, "The Uses of History," discusses the use of historical evidence by the *philosophes,* it also throws much light on Becker's own concept of history. In her chapters on Becker's ideas of history, Mrs. Smith devoted little attention to *The Heavenly City.* This was justified since Becker revealed his thought on the nature of history far more systematically in other writings. The whole series of lectures was not history in the conventional sense, nor was Becker pretending to write a history of eighteenth-century philosophy. He was dealing with the history of ideas, a field in which it is often more difficult to establish "historical facts" than in political, social, or economic history. Yet Becker's respect for factual accuracy is revealed once more in his reference to the significance of the publication date of Hume's *Dialogues.*

Becker's impatience with the minutiae of insignificant fact finding, an aspect of his historical relativism, is openly expressed in a passage omitted from page 142 of the book concerning "The Uses of Posterity." At the point where he refers to future generations who will "vindicate the Voltaires and Rousseaus, the Robespierres and the Rolands," Becker regrets, in the typed manuscript, the tendency of historians to be more concerned with whether Madame Roland had been executed on the eighth or the tenth of November, 1793, than with her opinions and influence. To Becker, preoccupied with Madame Roland's regard for the judgment of posterity and her influence during the French Revolution, the determination of whether she died on the eighth or two days later appeared of relative unimportance. Becker spent as much time on the study of the thought of a single *philosophe* as the mere chronicler does on establishing a historical date and by implication estimates the role of the historian of ideas far above that of the pedestrian chronicler. He quotes Hume, on page 95, to summarize the purpose of history: "Its chief use is only to discover the constant and universal principles of human nature."

Becker's relativism also underlay his contention that the *philosophes* were not the objective historians they aimed to be.[10] No one would quarrel with his assertions that the *philosophes* put a low estimate on the Middle Age, that they appealed to history rather than to metaphysical justification to fortify their attacks on abuses of the Old Regime, and that their arguments led to programs of reform. *The Heavenly City* furnished new fuel for the debate among historians over the relative importance of philosophy or of conditions as causes of the French Revolution, although this was certainly not Becker's conscious intention. By implying that the *philosophes* were not so revolutionary after all, Becker tended to reinforce the importance of the abuses and actual conditions in promoting revolution.

In 1933, when this challenge from Becker was first beginning to exert an influence, Ernest Labrousse published his two monumental volumes on the history of prices in eighteenth-century France.[11] These volumes were a closely reasoned text based on exhaustive statistical research (objective historical facts), but Labrousse also pointed out the social and political implications of his economic findings. The meeting on the French Revolution at the sessions of the American Historical Association in New York in 1940 was focused on the volumes of Labrousse,[12] and the one held in 1947 at Cleveland was

[10] *Supra*, 108–109.

[11] *Esquisse du mouvement des prix et des revenus en France au XVIIIe siècle* (2 vols.; Paris, 1933).

[12] At the 1947 session a paper by Louis Gottschalk was the basis of discussion by a panel composed of John Hall Stewart, Robert R. Palmer, and the author. At the New York session the author

devoted entirely to a discussion of the causes of the French Revolution. In the United States, where Becker had taught a whole school of French Revolutionary historians, such as Louis Gottschalk, Leo Gershoy, Geoffrey Bruun, John Hall Stewart, Robert R. Palmer, and others, historians of the eighteenth century and French Revolution tended to divide rather sharply into those who considered political, social, and economic conditions the prime factor and those who believed philosophy the main cause of the Revolution.

In France, however, where Becker's volume was little known, other works by French scholars on eighteenth-century philosophy appeared, and these combined with the Labrousse volumes led to a new synthesis of causes—that both the leavening influence of the *philosophes* and bad conditions (a sharp crisis) were necessary to bring about the revolutionary changes of 1789.

Although Becker's little volume and Labrousse's two big ones may be said to represent opposite poles of historical focus and method, both authors agreed on several points. Both implied the necessity of dividing the eighteenth century into two periods for correct appraisal of the causes of the French Revolution, and both were concerned with the divergence between eighteenth-century thought about conditions and the actual conditions, that is, the psychological factors in history. Neither Becker nor Labrousse was a determinist, although the latter's interest in economic history, statistics, and François

---

gave a paper on Labrousse's volumes, much of which appeared in an article, "Recent Work on the French Revolution," in the *American Historical Review*, XLVII (April, 1942).

Simiand's theories has led many to think that Labrousse was an economic determinist. Both historians would, however, defend the "determinism" of historical facts upon valid historical interpretation. It must be remembered that each was dealing with a different type of historical writing. Imagination is a necessary part of all historical work, but Becker was as ready as Labrousse to vindicate the importance of historical facts, whether philosophical or socioeconomic, in the interpretation of the historical past.

The role of relativity in human development had been enunciated by Einstein and was playing an important role in science in the 1930s, but it was barely being perceived in most other branches of learning. In his remarks on science and the *philosophes,* Becker was anticipating the growing importance of science and the history of science in present-day historical investigation. *The Heavenly City* may have popularized a remarriage of philosophy and history through its discussion of ideas, and a remarriage of history and literature through its readable style, but it was also prophetic of the broadening concept of history. Even before Becker's writing, history had ceased to be "past politics," but Becker's discussion of eighteenth-century ideas served notice once more that historical writing should embody a synthesis of all man's development. If Becker were alive to deliver the Storrs Lectures today, he would not say the same things as in 1931, but he would undoubtedly increase his emphasis upon the relationship of natural science to history. Philosophy and science are both aspects of man's development, but more and more attention is being focused in the 1950s on science. Becker's relativism in history may have seemed in the 1930s—and may seem to some to-day—to be a denial of history as social science and to be too close to speculative philosophy, but he was actually trying to demonstrate that great history is both a liberal art and a social science.

The third and, particularly, the last chapter of *The Heavenly City* deal with the idea of progress, the third with reference to the past and the final, to the future. The latter, entitled "The Uses of Posterity," is even less convincing to today's climate of opinion than to that of the depression-shocked early 1930s, whose mounting pessimism, fortified by a Second World War, has come to challenge the idea of material as well as philosophical and moral progress. The last lecture bore fewer changes in the typed text, and the few were more significant for Becker's conception of history than for the idea of progress. One has already been cited.[13]

In his discussion of the quarrel between the ancients and the moderns in the seventeenth century, Becker omitted from the printed text a rather long passage on the Age of Louis XIV that appears in the typed copy after the sentence listing defenders of the moderns, and before "It is sufficient to note that the ablest champion of the moderns, Fontenelle . . ."

Typed Manuscript	*Printed Version*
It is sufficient to note that with the beginning of the eighteenth century the notion of inevitable degeneration was already a thing of the past—no longer taken for	It is sufficient to note that the ablest champion of the moderns, Fontenelle, rested his defense upon the Cartesian doc-

[13] *Supra,* 103–104.

Typed Manuscript (cont.)

granted; it was possible to admire the age of Pericles without regarding it as superior to that of Louis XIV. That the superiority of the moderns should have been recognized in the late seventeenth and early eighteenth centuries is no mere coincidence. The splendor of the Sun King, the brilliance of his court, the luxury and finished perfection of social life, and the universal fame of French art and letters—all this could not but have seemed an obvious proof of the superiority of [break] contributed to the spread of the new doctrine. The Sun King did not easily tolerate invidious comparisons. We are told that everyone smiled when the king smiled, every one "was devout when the king was devout, and every one was sorry not to be ill when the king was ill." If it was criminal . . . [no page nos.; two separate pages].

Printed Version (cont.)

trine of the uniformity of nature. . . . [One page omitted.] To be oversanguine was characteristic of his generation; and if Fontenelle's theories were accepted it was less because of correct reasoning than because the age of Louis XIV was disposed to think well of itself. The Grand Monarch did not readily tolerate invidious comparisons. If it was criminal . . . [pp. 134 and 135–136].

Again, one can only speculate on the reasons why Becker eliminated this passage. Probably he recognized the exaggeration of the rejected phrases. The essential thought does appear in the text, and his remarks on Fontenelle and his own thesis regarding the *philosophes'* approach to the idea of progress gain by the omissions.

From Manuscript to Print

In the first section of the fourth chapter, Becker became involved in a discussion of the "specious present"—
a concept of philosophy at the very core of Becker's relativism. These passages, highly relevant to the historian,
are among the most ambiguous parts of the whole volume. What Becker was really portraying was the eighteenth century's rejection of the Christian doctrines of
the fall of man, salvation, and the day of judgment. A
short passage omitted from the printed text, in which
Becker was describing the Christian's faith in personal
salvation, further illuminates Becker's own climate of
opinion and that of the 1930s. The omitted passage appeared in the typed copy at the end of the long paragraph on page 127 of the printed text and just ahead of
the sentence beginning "Superficially considered, considered as an account of events historically verifiable, the
story was no doubt flimsy enough . . ."

This simple version of the drama of human destiny is so
unsuited to our climate of opinion that to us it seems but one
of many myths, and we are apt to wonder what could have
been the secret of its tenacious hold (even yet by no means
entirely broken) on the mind of men [no page no.].

This passage would have been an overt admission by
Becker that he did not believe in a future life and would
have turned the reader from attention to the eighteenth
century to his own day. In the printed text the paragraph that followed was skeptical but not agnostic. The
age of the New History was skeptical of the supernatural,
and rationalist Humanism was beginning to diverge much
farther from Christian doctrines than did eighteenth-
century deism.

Beatrice F. Hyslop

Critics of *The Heavenly City* would accept Becker's claim that the *philosophes* transferred their attention from a past Golden Age, whether of antiquity or of a Garden of Eden, to the attainment of perfection in the future. This future was not to be in another world after a day of judgment but would come about on earth in proportion as their ideas were put into practice.

Critics would be less ready to accept at face value Becker's analysis of French Revolutionary self-justification by appeal to the judgment of posterity. This thought was most clearly stated on pages 141–142:

The eighteenth-century revolutionists, whether in thought or in deed, responded to this need [for justification]. Finding themselves out of harmony with the temporary world of men and things, they endeavoured to put themselves in tune with the infinite powers: over against the ephemeral customs and mores, they set the universal laws of nature and of nature's God; from the immediate judgments of men, they appealed to the universal judgment of humanity.

The sentence about the date of the death of Madame Roland occurred in the typed text at the end of this paragraph. Becker may have overemphasized his point by using Madame Roland's memoirs or excerpts from Robespierre as typical of all French Revolutionary leaders, but both arguments reinforced his discussion of Diderot on posterity. Although optimism, deriving from confidence in a favorable judgment by subsequent generations, was a part of the thinking of influential French Revolutionary figures, historians might challenge the importance attached to this notion of posterity by Becker's last chapter.

From Manuscript to Print

The fourth section of "The Uses of Posterity" contains a description of the French Revolutionary religion of Liberty, Equality, and Fraternity, already referred to, and some comparison of the French and the Russian Revolutions. Readers of today would respond differently from those of the 1930s to this part of the book. When Becker delivered his lectures, the recognition of Soviet Russia by the United States was still two years off, and the best prophets would not have foreseen the purge trials of 1936, the Nazi-Soviet Pact of 1939, the Nazi invasion of Russia in 1941, and the consequent wartime alliance of the Western powers with Communist Russia. Becker admitted several times that he was using what the Soviets said about their revolution rather than what impartial historians wrote. In his treatment of the French Revolution and in his comparison of the two Revolutions, Becker was both reassessing liberalism and twitting the conservatives of his own day. As a genuine liberal, Becker would have condemned Communist developments of the 1950s, but he would also have condemned the use of his own basic ideas to bolster neoconservatism. The lectures end with a question of what posterity will be celebrating in 2032. "The Uses of Posterity" is one more proof that Becker would not have delivered the same lectures in 1957 as in 1931.

Comparison of the original typed text and the final printed words provides a small measure of clarification of the aims and the ideas Becker expressed in *The Heavenly City*. His purpose, his sincerity, and the tentative nature of the novel thesis he defended are all clearer. For the twentieth-century reader, with his own changing perspectives, the value of approaching eighteenth-century thought as a climate of opinion is sharpened. Becker's argument, which emphasizes Christian elements in deism and the relative unimportance of atheism in the thought of the *philosophes,* appears more convincing. Omissions in the printed text also help refine Becker's concept of history and of eighteenth-century optimism. The changes certainly illustrate Becker, the literary craftsman.

The Heavenly City has been read and will continue to be read for a variety of intellectual stimulations. Historians of philosophy, particularly of eighteenth-century thought and of the French Revolution, must read it. The historian will find in it important implications for an understanding of the nature of history. Both historian and layman can profit by reflection on the climate of opinion of past eras and of their own day. Whether Mr. Everyman is interested in history, philosophy, religion, or ethics, he will find on every page a challenge to his "faith," his "reason," and his basic ideas on religion, society, and humanity.

Carl Becker's volume will be read long after more conventional histories of eighteenth-century ideas have been forgotten. *The Heavenly City* merits a place among those relatively few volumes that are simultaneously creative in historical interpretation and challenging to the thoughtful reader.

R. R. PALMER

8. Thoughts on
The Heavenly City

The Heavenly City of the Eighteenth-Century Philosophers was published in the year I went to Cornell to do my graduate work with Carl Becker. It was an event in my own life, as was my whole association with Professor Becker; and it is with mixed feelings that I now, twenty-five years later, think back upon him and upon his book. The world has changed a good deal since 1932. And we change with it, as the Latin poet said. It is a long time since I have given any connected thought to philosophical matters, and I offer no systematic critique of *The Heavenly City*. It may be that the few autobiographical remarks with which I begin will be as illuminating as anything else I can contribute to the discussion.

I well remember the delight and admiration with which I first read the book, and reread it for a long time as I went over it with students. It seemed to me subtle, profound, slyly humorous, and beautifully written. I was struck by its exact workmanship, its fresh and independent judgments, its avoidance of the usual clichés on the eighteenth century, its freedom from any trace of the flat or commonplace in word or thought. I would like to think that the book had an influence on me. At any rate, the first thing I ever published was directly inspired by its concluding chapter. This was an article on "Posterity and the Hereafter in Eighteenth-Century France," which appeared in 1937. A certain impatience with the *philosophes,* or an inability to take them at their face value, which I found confirmed by *The Heavenly City,* supplied some of the motivation for my first book.[1] I apologize for saying these things, which I offer only as evidence of my very great indebtedness to Carl Becker. And I insist on acknowledging this indebtedness because I no longer feel quite the same enthusiasm for *The Heavenly City* that I once did.

The other day I reread it in preparation for the present symposium after not having looked at it for several years, during which I had felt estranged from its underlying philosophy. It again cast its old spell. It still seems to me a classic, a masterpiece, managing to run on several levels of discourse at the same time, with its vivid and amusing images, its mischievous ironies, its little character sketches and apt quotations which show the author's long familiarity with the people about whom he wrote. It is even, I would say, one of the finest pieces of literary art ever produced by a historian in America. This is not merely to say that it is well written—as I still think, apparently differing with Mr. Gottschalk [2]—though the

[1] *Catholics and Unbelievers in Eighteenth Century France* (Princeton, N.J., 1939).
[2] *Supra,* 89.

124

style is not one that anyone else should incautiously imitate. It is a work of art because so much of the author's own mood, personality, and view of the world is infused into its apparent subject matter. Originating as a series of lectures, the book remains a series of personal essays. Certainly Becker would never have thought that he had said the last word, or that his *The Heavenly City* should be the only or the principal work read by students on the eighteenth century; and certainly he would have been amused, more amused than anyone appears to be here today, at the thought of an assemblage of historians, disciples or others, meeting twenty-five years later for a grave reconsideration of this one work. I well remember the gusto with which, in a seminar, he once told how Karl Marx, surrounded by a group of talkative admirers, blurted out, "I am not a Marxist!"

His point, as we all know, was that the eighteenth century was in many ways much like the thirteenth, that what has been called the Age of Reason carried on, revived, or adapted many of the habits of mind, or the concern for saving humanity, that had animated the Age of Faith. There are two senses in which this point seems to me valid, or in which the interpretation seems to be "true," to use an un-Beckerish word. One sense is objective: it seems true to me, in a very general way, that only a society with a Christian background would have produced the eighteenth-century Enlightenment. It is unlikely that a Confucian or Hindu or Moslem or pagan society would ever have developed the characteristic belief of the Philosophers, that right knowledge of nature and history might improve the lot in this world of all men alike, or generated the impulse, the incentive, and the confidence to bring these improvements into being. At a high level of generalization, the proposition that the Enlightenment represented a secularization of medieval Christianity seems to me perfectly tenable. It is here, I think, that I differ with Mr. Gay.

The other sense in which the thesis of *The Heavenly City* is true is more subjective; that is, it is true within the framework of thought of Carl Becker. The more we accept this framework, the truer *The Heavenly City* will seem; and the less we accept it, the less so. The framework is that of an advanced case of historical relativism. It is a philosophy of skepticism, or disbelief in the possibility of objective knowledge, or of knowledge distinct from the taste, proclivities, interests, or prejudices of the knower. Becker, if I have understood him correctly, believed no more in "reason" than in ghosts. Men in this view cannot possess knowledge but only "ideas," and these ideas do not apprehend anything that is really "there" (or if they do we cannot tell it) but are concepts that we ourselves contrive or project out of our own mental states, needs, temperaments, desires, customs, or climate of opinion. Belief is only affirmation. If there is a plan or system of the world, a course of history, a nature or a human nature to which our thoughts or actions "ought" to conform, we can know nothing of them.

Seen from this point of view, the eighteenth and the thirteenth centuries were unquestionably much alike. Thomas Aquinas and Voltaire did both believe that there was a right knowledge of a real world, that they possessed some part of this knowledge, that men would be better off if they shared in such knowledge and acted accordingly, and would suffer if they did not. So much, I think, is true; but possibly only from a highly skeptical point of view is it an important affirmation. If we are not beset with philosophical doubt, if the problem of knowledge does not prey upon our minds, if we descend to more concrete levels, if we examine the society and institutions and actual felt problems and specific aspirations of people, then the difference between the two centuries begins to reappear. It indeed becomes very great. We may think, as Mr. Gay does, that the important thing about the Enlightenment is not how it echoes the thirteenth century but how it ushers in more modern times, including some of the more humane, liberal, equitable, and reasonably efficient institutions considered desirable in many countries ever since.

The interesting problem, then, raised by *The Heavenly City*, is not whether its picture of the eighteenth century is valid, but whether we are to accept the philosophical position that gives it such validity as it has. There has been a considerable reaction against historical relativism since the 1930s. Since Hitler, and the Soviet rewriting of history, and the warnings of George Orwell, we are less inclined than we were in the 1930s (and I include myself) to agree that historical knowledge, or any alleged knowledge, is only an affirmation that satisfies him who affirms it.

You will not, I hope, take me for a religious revivalist if I cite *The Screwtape Letters*, where the impish Screwtape boasts that the Historical Point of View is an invention of the devil. The Historical Point of View, he explains to his henchman, consists in this: that we never ask of an idea whether it is true or false, right or wrong (on the plea that we cannot know), but only state that so-and-so entertained the idea, that he derived it from such-and-such sources, that it resembled certain other ideas, that others were influenced by his idea or quoted it or readapted it for some other purpose, that many people shared the idea or that few did, that it flourished and succeeded or withered and died away. Now I fear that we historians are in fact pretty much limited to this unholy business, but I do not see that we need to make a philosophy and a program of it. And I am afraid that my mentor, Carl Becker, in 1932 had fallen into the clutches of Screwtape. The importance of Christianity, he observes, was that "it announced with authority (whether truly or not matters little) that the life of man has significance" (p. 128). And of the ideas of the *philosophes* he declares it "not possible" to estimate the "value of their philosophy, to tell wherein it is true, wherein false. . . . Living in the twentieth century, I am limited by the preconceptions of my age. It was therefore inevitable that I should approach the subject from the historical point of view" (p. 28).

There are a number of implications here with which I can no longer comfortably agree: that any man need be wholly limited by "preconceptions of his age"; that there is a pervasive, compelling climate of opinion shaping the whole content of any individual mind; that any line of thought is "inevitable," or inevitable for this reason; that, if this is the historical point of view, the historian can or should be content to be a historian merely. Surely, if we spend much of our lives thinking about the eighteenth century, the validity of its ideas or lack of validity, or the shades between, and the conditions and requisites and implications of validity are matters that we should always keep somewhere in mind.

The disinclination to discuss the validity (that is, the truth or right) of an idea, or the belief that there can be no rational basis for exchange of views on such questions, may have been a carry-over, in Becker's relativism, from the older positivist or scientific schools of history of which his own relativist ideas were a critique. It may have arisen also from a certain aesthetic element in his historical theory. By this I only mean that he seems to have valued history as an observer of the human scene, finding in it a chance to savor, to experience, to relive, to re-enact the human adventure—or, indeed, to have something interesting to write about. He lacked the political involvement of Beard (and was thus doubtless saved from many excesses), as he lacked Beard's concern for a historical or social science. Every age, said Becker, must "make the dead perform whatever tricks it finds necessary for its own peace of mind" (p. 44). To have an explanation means that we have attained "mental satisfaction" or "a restful conclusion." Of course, Becker was too troubled and deep a man to attach any superficial meaning to "peace of mind" or "restful conclusions." He spoke philosophically, as a philosopher. Still, these are strange concepts to bring to bear on the *philosophes* of the eighteenth century. The truths of which the *philosophes* felt so confident gave them no peace of mind, at least in France; nor were their conclusions very restful, even if we are referring only to their own inner psychology. For one who has so often been called a pragmatist, it is strange that Becker, in *The Heavenly City*, did not put more emphasis on the social utility of eighteenth-century ideas. Historical ideas, like other ideas, do have a practical application and originate to some extent under practical pressures, as means used to diagnose the causes of felt grievances, or to envisage proposed solutions to felt problems, or to advance or reconcile divergent interests, or to persuade groups of men to collective action by offering a common ground of understanding, purpose, or hope. Becker would have denied none of this; had he followed this line he would have written a different book on the eighteenth century. It would not have been *The Heavenly City*, for the resemblance between eighteenth- and thirteenth-century thought patterns would have been noted as no more than incidental, but it might have been a book more relevant to our own time.

Perhaps the chief secondary thesis in *The Heavenly City* is the argument that the *philosophes*, regretfully concluding that nature gave no foundation for a difference between right and wrong, turned to history in the pursuit of this same quest and from comparison of various societies and forms of behavior sought to distinguish "man in general" (as a norm of the good or right) from men as modified by various customs and environments, most of which were judged to have had a bad effect. This is a brilliant intuition and may be true; I doubt if it can be proved or disproved by evidence. It is certain that the *philosophes* did dwell at great length on "man in general," natural man, humanity, and the human species. One reason why they did so, in my opinion, is not that they found cosmic or physical nature devoid of norms, but that they found the society and institutions of their time increasingly artificial, "unnat-

ural," and constricting. The problem, as I see it, is not to
derive ideas from other ideas, or one century from another century, but to examine the ideas in their close
social context and with regard to what can be known of
the psychology of human beings. As for "man in general,"
so ridiculed by De Maistre and the counterrevolutionary
schools of the nineteenth century, the search for him is
after all still going on, though the terminology has pretty
well disguised that fact. The aim of psychology, soci-
ology, and other such pursuits, one would suppose, is
precisely to establish generalizations that are not limited
to any particular milieu and which offer a common
ground on which particular patterns of behavior or social
organization may be understood, evaluated, or compared.

We have lived now for forty years in an age shaken by
revolutions, and such also was the eighteenth century, or
its latter half. I do not, to tell the truth, any longer find
much in *The Heavenly City* to explain the phenomenon
of revolution. Nor, perhaps, should one expect to, in a
sense; for Becker's basic ideas were formed before the
First World War, and he was forty-four years old when
Lenin led the revolution of 1917. We can accept, as a
certain mood of the 1930s, the closing paragraphs of *The
Heavenly City*, with their comparison of the Russian
Revolution to the French and their hopeful prognosis
that communism will one day seem as innocuous as re-
publicanism. In its early years the book had a certain
vogue among liberals. I believe Mr. Gay is right in ob-
serving that today it suits the "neoconservatives."

Anyone forming his idea of the French Enlightenment
and the French Revolution from this book alone (as, of

course, Becker never intended that anyone should)
would quite possibly reach these conclusions: [that the
idea of improving society was a "faith," or even a delusion, for which no rational evidence could be offered;
that such an idea arose only from other ideas, rather than
from dislocations and defects in existing society, or from
wants, needs, frustrations, or practical demands among
people other than writers; that the Revolution thus had
no legitimate or actual cause, so to speak, other than a
fermentation of minds; that the program of the *philosophes* was a "utopian dream of perfection," an attempt to
build heaven on earth; that the extremes to which the
Revolution went were due to the boundless optimism of
revolutionaries, rather than to resistance and conflict;
that the Revolution was a hysteria, and that its essence
was revealed on the day when Robespierre pontificated
at the Worship of the Supreme Being; that the Reign of
Terror was a mad attempt to apply "philosophy" to real
life, rather than a mortal struggle between two sides,
each bent on the other's total destruction, and both
aroused less by "ideas" than by elemental emotions of
loyalty and dedication, fear and hate. This, to be brief, is
not the light in which I have come to see the eighteenth
century or the great turmoil in which it ended.

But perhaps all such comments are beside the point.
With much of what I have said I do not think that
Becker would have greatly disagreed. He might justly
remark that his own purpose was different. I have already
said that *The Heavenly City* is a work of art; I have heard
others at this conference observe that it is really not a
work of history at all. I would not go so far; it is a work
of history, but at the same time more than history. I re-

member his once remarking to me, as we left his lecture
and crossed the campus to Boardman Hall, that history
was after all "an inferior form of thought," that the great
poets and novelists had more to say. *The Heavenly City*
is more than a history because it is the expression of a
rare and gifted mind, of one who had suffered, who had
honestly wrestled with life's hardest questions, and who
had accepted no facile answers. For such a mind the
usual exercises of the historian no longer seemed very
rewarding. Like Marcus Aurelius, whom he quotes at
the end of the book, he felt that a man of forty years, if
also a man of sense, knew as much as he ever would know
of what had been or could be.

GUSSIE E. GASKILL

CORNELL UNIVERSITY LIBRARY

9. "Here Is This Little Book"

CARL BECKER says in *The Heavenly City:* "And how often it happens that books 'influence' readers in ways not intended by the writers!" [1] It seems this has been the fate of *The Heavenly City.* Certainly the author did not intend it to be a textbook or treatise on eighteenth-century thought. On the contrary, he assumed that his readers would already know a good deal about the *philosophes* and their work and the period in which they lived. Having been greatly attracted by them, he himself had read widely and deeply in their writings and in what others had written about them for years, and over the years he had thought a great deal about them and their ideas. After these years of reading and thinking, he wrote the book to say some things about these eighteenth-century Philosophers which he thought needed to be said and to ask some questions which he thought needed to be asked. He wrote clearly because, as his colleague George Lincoln Burr once said, he thought clearly. He wrote with a light touch and a quizzical and gentle, or

[1] Page 73.

134

maybe not always so gentle, humor, because it was not in him to be solemn about anything, certainly not about his own ideas. If the result of his writing the way he, being himself, had to write is a book so charming and persuasive that it has "influenced" a great many readers in ways not intended by the writer, well, that's too bad. But it's not the first time it has happened and won't be the last.

There is no question about Becker's taking the book seriously. He took everything he wrote seriously, if one means by that that he said what he meant to say as clearly and as well as he could. When he gave me a copy of *The Heavenly City,* he said that when he was invited to come to Cornell—that was some fifteen years earlier— he had said that he was not a great scholar like Burr and Hull but that he hoped to write something some day about eighteenth-century philosophy. "And now," he added, "after all these years, here is this little book." As if he had written nothing else in all those years! In a letter of November 10, 1932, to Louis Gottschalk, he wrote: "I think it is the best of my books—the best constructed, the best thought out, the best written."

When the lectures were delivered at Yale, they were apparently entitled, *The Heavenly City of the Philosophes.* The Yale committee which approved their publication thought the title should be changed, but Mr. Becker insisted that it stand, except for the change from *"philosophes"* to "eighteenth-century philosophers," to which he must have agreed. He wrote: "The title seems to me a peculiarly happy one. It was suggested of course by the famous book of St. Augustine, 'The City of God'; and the sum and substance of the lectures is to show that the Philosophes of the eighteenth century formulated a social and political philosophy which took over the cardinal preconceptions of the Christian philosophy as formulated in St. Augustine's work. The lectures are carefully built up around this idea, and many parts of the ms. would be ambiguous and irrelevant if a different title should be used. The title is moreover one that suggests in a striking way the central thesis of the lectures; and one that will be entirely intelligible to the readers of the book, who will be for the most part scholars who are quite familiar with [the] phrase Heavenly City which St. Augustine made famous. For my part I cannot think of any good reason for changing the title." [2]

It seems to me that what Mr. Becker is saying in the book is, quite simply, that the eighteenth-century belief that through the laws of nature mankind could attain to a utopia is a faith just as was the earlier faith in the attainment of Heaven through God. He does not call the *philosophes* Christians but only recognizes the fact that many of their ideals were based on Christian teachings. In the end, moreover, he recognizes the similarities of the new faith in communism to the earlier faiths. He wrote the book not to disparage the *philosophes*, who were, as Mr. Gay quite rightly puts it, his intellectual forebears, not to accuse them of being naïve—he says

[2] Draft of a letter of Jan. 15, 1932, to Mr. Norman V. Donaldson of the Yale University Press, at the top of which in Mr. Becker's handwriting is the note: "Substance of the letter sent. Actual letter differently phrased in some parts." Both this draft and the letter to Mr. Gottschalk are in the Becker papers in the Cornell University Archives, and I am grateful to Phil L. Snyder, assistant archivist, for bringing them to me.

136

that Voltaire was an optimist "although not a naïve one" [3] —not because he was impatient with them, let alone considering them even a little fraudulent, but because, looking back over the couple of centuries that had passed since their time, he questioned the validity of their faith, as he did that of any faith in the betterment of the condition of man through natural or supernatural laws. Nine years later in his lectures at the University of Virginia, he stated the same thought affirmatively when he said that it is "futile to rely upon the saving grace of some transcendent increasing purpose (a law of nature, or dialectic of history, or totalitarian state), to bring us in spite of ourselves to a predestined good end." [4]

[3] *Heavenly City*, 37.
[4] *Modern Democracy* (New Haven, 1941), 100.

PART III

The Reassessment:
The Symposium in Perspective

RALPH H. BOWEN

NEW YORK STATE UNIVERSITY
COLLEGE ON LONG ISLAND

10. *The Heavenly City:*
A Too-ingenious Paradox

CARL BECKER'S book about the eighteenth-century Philosophers is nearly as difficult to write about as it is easy to read. The odds are, in the first place, that any commentary will be less lively and less persuasive than the original. To praise it seems superfluous, considering the large number who are already convinced that it is a masterpiece. To find fault with it seems, by the same token, presumptuous or—in view of its many merits—ungracious. The book and its thesis must be taken seriously because of Becker's stature as a historian and because of the tremendous influence his book has had, particularly in America, on thinking about the Enlightenment. Yet too much solemnity might well be dangerous, for it is entirely possible that Becker had his tongue in his cheek a good part of the time. One more than half suspects that in a number of places he was mischievously indulging his well-known taste for paradox and that more than anything else he was trying to stir people up in order to start them thinking.

This ability of Becker's to overcome the inertia of other minds was, of course, one of the qualities that made him such a superb teacher, and it is surely one of the most substantial merits of *The Heavenly City* that it has made a whole generation of students re-examine the *philosophes* in a more critical spirit. The book still retains, after twenty-five years, nearly all of its remarkable power to provoke fruitful controversy. I suppose Becker would regard this fact as ample justification for having written *The Heavenly City*.

But I also believe that the last thing Carl Becker wanted was to have his readers swallow without question the whole thesis of *The Heavenly City*. I think he would be intensely unhappy to see how often his book is taken for a final judgment on the nature and meaning of the Enlightenment—something it most certainly is not and probably was never intended to be. I think he would be especially displeased to know how often college teachers ignorantly or irresponsibly recommend *The Heavenly City* to beginning students as "a splendid short account of eighteenth-century thought."

Becker's Yale lectures, the original version of *The Heavenly City*, were addressed to an audience that could be presumed to be fairly well informed about the eighteenth century. He may well have taken it for granted that he was under no obligation to recite the elementary facts which every schoolboy should—but usually doesn't— know about the *philosophes*. Instead he seems to have tried mainly to suggest new ways of interpreting some of that information. He apparently felt little need to guard against misunderstandings because he assumed that his audience knew what he was doing and would not mistake his frankly tentative suggestions for a balanced treatment of the whole subject. No more would one expect an audience of West Pointers to mistake a series of lectures on the tactics of trench warfare for a definitive military history of the First World War. Yet a mistake of approximately this magnitude resulted from the publication of Becker's lectures in book form.

The new audience was large and miscellaneous and mostly unsophisticated. Becker must have been aware of this, and it is puzzling that he apparently made no special effort to prevent confusion. Perhaps he did not expect the book to have anything like the sensational popularity which it soon achieved and hence did not at first see any need to take precautions. It almost certainly did not occur to him that his professional colleagues would be the first to fall into the blunder of taking *The Heavenly City* for more than it pretended to be. Yet, beginning with the reviewers for the learned journals, this is precisely what happened. Becker might, of course, have protested in print, although he could hardly have done so at that point without causing embarrassment. One must concede, too, that it is a rare thing for an author to take exception to favorable reviews. Furthermore, there was still no convincing proof that a significant number of persons was relying solely on *The Heavenly City* for elementary knowledge about the *philosophes*. It has taken nearly a quarter of a century for this deplorable state of affairs to become fully evident, though I do not think that even now the average college teacher is aware of the true magnitude of the problem.

Ralph H. Bowen

These reflections are largely the product of my own experience over the past ten years in assigning *The Heavenly City* as collateral reading in undergraduate courses. No other book is so uniformly misunderstood. Even when they are warned in advance that they may expect to find many debatable judgments in the book, the most able and mature students are often so charmed by its literary perfection that they drop their critical defenses and end by accepting Becker's shakiest hypotheses as a new revelation. I can sympathize with them because the same thing starts to happen to me every time I pick up the book to reread it. Becker had the dangerous gift of being able to make utter nonsense sound completely plausible. The central thesis of *The Heavenly City* is not pure nonsense by any means, but much of it is either wrong or irrelevant.

For when all is said and done, the plain truth of the matter is that the *philosophes* wanted to build an earthly city and not a heavenly one. No amount of wit can in the end obscure the momentous difference between the devout rationalism of the thirteenth century and the critical rationalism of the eighteenth. The *philosophes* accepted nothing on faith except reason itself, while the Schoolmen had found reasons for accepting nearly everything on faith. The eighteenth century's commitment to free inquiry and to free discussion stands in irreducible contrast to the medieval commitment to finality and uniformity of belief. There is a real difference and a very great one between Augustine's view of man's capacities and the view that most eighteenth-century thinkers held. It may be that Becker thought he had taken account of that difference when he inserted the phrase "allowance made for certain important alterations in the bias" in the formal statement of his thesis,[1] but I believe that if *sufficient* allowance is made for these "alterations in the bias," the effect is to cancel out altogether his main assertion that "the underlying preconceptions of eighteenth-century thought were still . . . essentially the same as those of the thirteenth century."[2]

The Heavenly City is often a brilliantly provocative interpretation of eighteenth-century ideas, but it is not always a well-informed one. Becker had certainly read widely in the classics of the Enlightenment, but his knowledge of some of the important European writers was far from encyclopedic and it was sometimes inaccurate. One can find in *The Heavenly City*, along with the perceptive comments that are justly admired, dozens of misconceptions, dubious generalizations, rhetorical exaggerations, erroneous citations, and factual mistakes. Many of these are trivial, but some of them are important. I shall mention only a few of the more serious.

He accepts the thoroughly exploded myth about Galileo's supposed use of the leaning tower of Pisa to measure the acceleration of gravity.[3] His remarks on the status of "enthusiasm" in eighteenth-century discussions[4] betray his unfamiliarity with a whole current of feeling and opinion, the one stemming from Shaftesbury and counting Diderot as its most eminent representative. His assertion that the *philosophes* were "the secular bearers of the Protestant and Jansenist tradition"[5] is doubly unfortunate—first, in implying that there was one tradition rather than two and, second, in ignoring the obvious fact

---

[1] *Heavenly City*, 31.   [2] *Ibid.*   [3] *Ibid.*, 20.
[4] *Ibid.*, 37.   [5] *Ibid.*, 42.

that the only important element common to both Jan-senism and Protestantism was the Augustinian idea of original sin: this idea, as Cassirer emphasizes,[6] was vir-tually the only one unanimously opposed by "enlight-ened" thinkers no matter what their tendency or shade of opinion. Becker's appraisal of Raynal's *Philosophical and Political History of European Settlement and Commerce in the Two Indies* is grossly unfair to Raynal in calling his book "half fiction" and in implying that Raynal de-liberately twisted facts to suit his beliefs.[7]

Occasionally Becker contrives a bit of startlingly per-verse logic like this one: "The Philosophers were, after all, primarily concerned with the present state of things, which they wished to change; and they needed good reasons for their desire to change it."[8] Surely the order of events is here inverted, unless Becker meant to say that the Philosophers' desire for change was in the be-ginning utterly without reasons, hence completely capri-cious and irrational, needing to be supported by reasons invented after the event. Perhaps this is his real meaning, but if it is, the point is of sufficient importance to be dis-cussed at length—after all, people do not often set out to change an existing state of things without any good reason. Yet Becker merely goes on to list the reasons which he supposes the Philosophers to have invented *ex post facto*.

There is a small grain of truth and a mountain of exag-geration in the statement that "the eighteenth-century Philosophers held fast to a revealed body of knowledge,

[6] Ernst Cassirer, *The Philosophy of the Enlightenment* (Prince-ton, N.J., 1951), 141.
[7] *Heavenly City*, 110.   [8] *Ibid.*, 140.

and they were unwilling or unable to learn anything from history which could not be reconciled with their faith." [9] The grain of truth is, of course, to be found in the valid but trite observation that the historians of the Enlightenment—like their confrères in other ages—were not always free of unconscious bias. But the remainder of the statement is overdrawn to the point of becoming a caricature. From Bayle and Voltaire through Robertson, Hume, and Gibbon there is—in addition to a candidly avowed and easily discounted point of view—overwhelming evidence of a growing passion for accuracy, completeness, and impartiality, as well as an increasing willingness to hew to the facts, let the philosophical chips fall where they may. Becker probably did not mean to provide such a spectacular example of Voltaire's saying that "History is a pack of tricks played on the dead," nor did the historians of the Enlightenment deserve to have such a trick played at their expense.

Becker correctly emphasizes that the idea of natural law was the most fundamental of the "underlying preconceptions" on which eighteenth-century thought rested. And in his second chapter he rightly makes much of the fact that "in the eighteenth-century climate of opinion, . . . nature is the test, the standard." [10] He has many acute things to say about the religion of nature which enabled the disciples of the Newtonian philosophy to go on worshipping after they had given "another form and a new name to the object of worship: having denatured God, they deified nature." [11] But it is not clear how this point furthers his general argument, for Becker's thesis asserts an identity between the objects of worship

[9] *Ibid.*, 102.　　　[10] *Ibid.*, 53.　　　[11] *Ibid.*, 63.

of the eighteenth century and those of the thirteenth century. It is not enough for his purpose to show that religious feelings were present and important in both ages, for Becker had undertaken to show that the *philosophes* were really Christians, and medieval Christians at that. Unless he meant to contend that all religions are "essentially" identical, he was obliged to show that nature worship is really the same thing as Christianity and not a heresy, as Christian theologians have always maintained. Becker does none of these things. His argument marches part way up the hill, proclaims that it has reached the summit, and then marches unobtrusively down again. I do not know whether Becker was aware of this logical hiatus or whether he was taken in by his own verbal pyrotechnics.

A similar confusion, or sleight of hand, appears in his discussion of natural law. Becker is prompt to admit that concepts of nature and natural law antedate both the Enlightenment and Christianity. Then, however, he sweeps all pre-Christian versions of natural law under the rug: "In the earlier centuries the ideal image of nature was, as one may say, too ghostly ever to be mistaken for nature herself." Becker is apparently speaking here only of the medieval image of nature, for the Greeks had not found nature "intractable, even mysterious and dangerous, at best inharmonious to man"; [12] neither had the Stoic philosophers, who transmitted the idea of natural law to Christian thought.

He leaves us to conclude that allegiance to natural law is one of the important "preconceptions" that the eighteenth and the thirteenth centuries had in common.

[12] *Ibid.*, 55.

Nowhere does he explicitly draw this conclusion—perhaps he was wise to let it appear only by indirection. At any rate, he was probably aware that it would seriously weaken his argument to point out what is surely an obvious feature of the Enlightenment: that its concept of nature and natural law was sharply opposed to the Christian concept and closely allied to the ancient Stoic notion. Here, as on so many other fundamental issues, Becker adroitly suggests the false while suppressing the true. The *philosophes* must at all costs be proved to be medieval Christians, even if rhetoric has to be substituted for logic in the process.

Detailed criticism of Becker's third chapter would also call attention to a number of serious misstatements, incorrect or misleading references, and erroneous interpretations. These slips are more abundant in this section, for some reason, than in the remainder of the book. The worst distortions occur in the discussions of Montesquieu and Diderot. Space is not available to deal systematically with these distortions, but those which appear in a single paragraph devoted to Diderot may be noted as typical.[13] "Diderot . . . is often classed with the atheists," says Becker; and he goes on to call Diderot "this atheist, convinced against his will." It would be more accurate to describe Diderot as an agnostic, and the weight of specialist opinion supports this interpretation. Becker's next sentence contains a puzzling error of fact: he cites *"La Physiologie"* as one of Diderot's "speculative works" —but the allusion can only be to some rough notes made by Diderot while reading Haller's treatise on physiology; a few of these notes contain Diderot's own ideas, but

[13] *Ibid.*, 79–80.

by no stretch of the imagination can these notebooks be considered an original "speculative work." The other work cited is presumably *D'Alembert's Dream*, though it is referred to only as "*L'Entretien*" and Diderot wrote several pieces whose titles begin with that word. In this same sentence there appears a misquotation from *D'Alembert's Dream*. According to Becker's text, Diderot "reached the conclusion that . . . good will is nothing but 'the last impulse of desire and aversion' "; Diderot's own text is: "The sense of free will . . . is simply the most recent impulse of desire or aversion." [14] I have nowhere found Diderot saying, as Becker would have him say, that "vice and virtue are mere words signifying nothing," though it is easy enough to find him saying the opposite. Finally, the next two sentences contain a misstatement of fact. "Diderot the rationalist wrote these works. But there was another Diderot who refused to publish them." There was never any question of a *refusal* to publish. The notes on Haller were never meant for publication; d'Alembert refused to allow the publication of *D'Alembert's Dream* because the dialogue gave offense to his friend, Julie de Lespinasse. Diderot never had any objection to the limited publication of his dialogue in Grimm's *Correspondance littéraire*, and it did in fact appear there in 1782, two years before Diderot's death. The remainder of the paragraph contains a debatable account of *Rameau's Nephew*, but this is less disturbing than the series of demonstrable mistakes on which the main argument of the paragraph is based.

The concluding chapter on "The Uses of Posterity" is probably the best. Becker here comes closest to being

[14] *Rameau's Nephew and Other Works of Diderot*, trans. by Jacques Barzun and Ralph Bowen (New York, 1956), 166.

right about the *philosophes*. The trouble is that he also
does irreparable damage to his own contention that the
philosophes were unconscious Christians. We cannot
agree with this thesis if we accept Becker's very cogent
demonstration that they substituted posterity for the traditional Christian belief in personal immortality. For
how many Christians—especially medieval Christians—
have thought that worldly reputation is an adequate
recompense for the loss of the soul's salvation? Diderot
and his friends did indeed believe that "posterity is for
the philosopher what the other world is for the religious
man," and if it were not for the hypnotic power of Becker's prose one would think that this fact alone would
serve to give some measure of the gulf that divides the
eighteenth-century Philosophers from the Christian rationalists of the thirteenth century. The *philosophes* were,
no doubt, religious in some senses of the word, and
Becker is correct—if somewhat redundant—in insisting
on this point. What he fails to take into account is that
one can very easily be religious without being a Christian
and that one can be Christian without being an Augustinian.

To summarize the foregoing discussion, it seems to
me that *The Heavenly City* suffers from two major defects: it often makes irresponsible use of evidence; and
it does not always establish a chain of logic between the
evidence adduced and the propositions to be demonstrated. The result is that either these propositions stand
on a shaky foundation of dubious fact and still more
dubious generalization or they are refuted by Becker's
own evidence once it is logically construed and evaluated.

This does not mean that *The Heavenly City* is a tissue

of error and illogic from start to finish. On the contrary, it is full of telling aphorisms and wonderfully acute observations which, taken singly, can only be enthusiastically applauded. The point is that most of these have no logical bearing on Becker's central paradox. They make *The Heavenly City* a lively, informative, perceptive book—probably the most provocative ever written about the Enlightenment. It is a pity that it is so often mistaken or irrelevant.

It is a pity, too, that Becker worked so hard in some places to be amusing. He was a master of epigram and of deft characterization. It is all the more regrettable that he so often chose, for rhetorical effect, to adopt a highly objectionable tone of condescending superiority to the men he was writing about. It seems not to have occurred to him that any of his own ideas might be thought naïve; yet the burden of his indictment of the Philosophers is that they were overcredulous:

These skeptics who eagerly assent to so much strike our sophisticated minds as overcredulous. We feel that they are too easily persuaded, that they are naïve souls after all, duped by their humane sympathies, on every occasion hastening to the gate to meet and welcome platitudes and panaceas. And so our jaded and somewhat morbid modern curiosity is at last aroused. We wish to know the reason for all this fragile optimism. We wish to know what it is that sustains this childlike faith, what unexamined prepossessions enable the Philosophers to see the tangled wilderness of the world in this symmetrical, this obvious and uncomplicated pattern.[15]

What entitles Becker to use this patronizing tone? Evidently some conviction of superior insight, of a more

[15] *Heavenly City,* 45–46.

sophisticated mind. If we try to find out where this conviction could have come from, we speedily discover that Becker makes the same gratuitous assumption that he ridicules the Philosophers for having made: he assumes that the philosophical fashions of his own day afford final standards of validity by which to judge the beliefs of all earlier ages. Thus he arrogates to himself and his own contemporaries an infallibility that he thinks ludicrous and pitiable when he finds it claimed by eighteenth-century writers. He is filled with respect for the quantum theory, for Freud, Whitehead, Russell, and—J. H. Jeans! He was at least as awestruck by the quantum theory as Voltaire ever was by Newton's philosophy, and an impartial critic might well conclude that both he and Voltaire were far too eager to draw metaphysical conclusions from current scientific developments.

As an intellectual historian Becker should have been acutely aware of the absurdity of most past attempts to transfer the findings or the methods of physical science to the social or moral realms. Yet he fell headlong into this very trap when he wrote that "the conclusions of modern science" compel us to regard man as "a chance deposit on the surface of the world, carelessly thrown up between two ice ages by the same forces that rust iron and ripen corn." [16] He should have known that the conclusions of science do not compel us to believe anything of the sort any more than the conclusions of Newtonian science compelled the eighteenth-century Philosophers to believe in deism.

I suspect that Carl Becker's real quarrel with the Philosophers arose out of his disappointment at finding that

[16] *Ibid.,* 14.

they were not actually such cynics as he had been brought up to believe. He belonged to a generation that was hypersensitive to buncombe and humbug in all its forms, possibly because it was ashamed at having been duped by war propaganda, and it often seemed to delight in parading its disillusionments. To many of Becker's contemporaries, faith of any sort was an unforgivable lapse, the hallmark of H. L. Mencken's boob. Becker, I think, was speaking for and to the nineteen-twenties when he concluded that "we" agree with the Philosophers "more readily when they are witty and cynical than when they are wholly serious. Their negations rather than their affirmations enable us to treat them as kindred spirits." [17]

At any rate, *The Heavenly City* seems to me essentially an expression of Becker's own disillusionment, not to say despair, disguised as an urbane attack on the naïveté of the Philosophers. Simple-mindedness, indeed, forms almost the entire burden of his accusation. They meant well, but they were too credulous—that is, not cynical enough. Voltaire's wit was "too *superficially* cynical to be more than a counterirritant." [18] The Philosophers' aversion to enthusiasm "did not carry them to the high ground of indifference" [19]—one might well ask why indifference should occupy high rather than low ground —and the projects of eighteenth-century reformers are dismissed with a scornful sneer: they are "naïvely simple" [20] or "futile." [21] Later, during the Revolution, their enthusiasm for liberty, justice, truth and humanity "becomes a delirium." [22] By contrast, two thoroughgoing

[17] *Ibid.*, 30.   [18] *Ibid.*, 36; my emphasis.   [19] *Ibid.*, 37.
[20] *Ibid.*, 40.   [21] *Ibid.*, 41.   [22] *Ibid.*, 43.

cynics, Frederick II (whom Becker several times refers to as "the great Frederick") and La Rochefoucauld are mentioned with respect because they took a dim, and therefore presumably sophisticated, view of man's prospects.

It is impossible to avoid the suspicion that Becker had a deep-seated animus of some sort against the *philosophes*. The epithets fly thick and fast, the invective is merciless and sustained; innuendo completes the task of demolition wherever logic leaves part of the work undone. We are finally convinced that Becker must have had a heavy score to settle with the Philosophers, for his tone is strikingly like that of the diatribes which some ex-Communists of our own day have directed against Soviet Russia. Had Becker shared the faith of the eighteenth century before twentieth-century developments seemed to make that faith rationally untenable—seemed, indeed, to make faith in reason itself an anachronism? Was Becker taking revenge on the *philosophes* for his own youthful naïveté and subsequent painful disillusionment? Does this account for his emotional intensity? Was Carl Becker unable to do justice to the Enlightenment because for him it was "the god that failed"?

JOHN HALL STEWART

WESTERN RESERVE UNIVERSITY

11. Thoughts
and Afterthoughts

WHEN I was invited to amplify, in a brief essay, the comments I had made and the questions I had posed at the Colgate symposium on Carl Becker's *The Heavenly City of the Eighteenth-Century Philosophers,* I was somewhat nonplussed. My remarks had seemed more or less obvious under the circumstances—in fact, I felt that if I had not made them someone else would have done so. Moreover, they were sufficiently discursive as to preclude the possibility of integrating them in any really intelligible synthesis. Accordingly, I have taken the liberty of presenting simply some thoughts (or afterthoughts) on the symposium as a whole. If in so doing I am able to utilize my comments and questions of the moment, I shall endeavor to make the most of them at the appropriate time and place.

We, a group of professional, academic historians, had assembled, as guests of the New York State Association of European Historians, at Colgate University to discuss problems of mutual interest. By the accident of circumstance, the principal topic chosen for the occasion was a timely and provocative one—"Carl Becker's *Heavenly City* Revisited Twenty-five Years After." What could be a more attractive or stimulating subject for a group which had once numbered Carl Becker among its most esteemed members? What could be a more fitting choice than *The Heavenly City*, the work which had come to be the most widely acclaimed of the many products of his fluent and facile pen?

Apart from two papers scheduled for the luncheon and dinner sessions of the conference, the major task of "revisiting" was to be done in two lengthy meetings, one in the morning ("The Critique"), the other in the afternoon ("The Reassessment"). The Critique was to be the work mainly of a generation that had not studied with Becker and that could know him only by hearsay or through his writings; the Reassessment was assigned to a panel, most of whom were distinguished students, friends, and admirers of Becker. To me this appeared to be the most appealing feature of the program, for it suggested a sort of 1956 battle of "Ancients" and "Moderns." (In the following pages I shall use these terms, not in any disparaging sense, but simply as a convenient device for differentiating between the "pros" and the "cons.")

At the outset the critics freely admitted that *The Heavenly City* was (and I cite without benefit of reference) probably the most urbane and doubtless the most influential monograph on European history published in this country within the last quarter-century; that it was a rare work of scholarship in that it was also a work of art; that its success was indicated by the fact that it had

157

gone through ten printings; and that it had done more than any other single work to shape present concepts of the Enlightenment. Thereafter, however, admissions of excellence yielded to the critical analysis of specialists.

In essence the conclusions of the Moderns might be summed up somewhat as follows: the book had never before been subjected to a really penetrating, scholarly examination; its "playful formulations" had been accepted uncritically by thousands of readers, many of whom seemed to have taken the writer's jests too seriously and his admonitions of caution too lightly; for that matter, Becker himself probably did not take the book too seriously. Nor was this all. To them it appeared that he had been guilty of sins of omission and commission that rendered the success of the work unmerited and even reflected unfavorably upon his professional integrity. For he had manifested "the fallacy of spurious persistence"; he had urged his readers to ask searching questions but continually suggested the wrong answers. Although he was certainly no conservative, the conservative implications of the book were so plain as to give comfort to the New Conservatives of our own day. His estimate of the *philosophes* had every virtue save the virtue of being right; he had erred, not only in attributing too much to Newton, but in misinterpreting the concept and influence of natural law. As a whole, his research was inadequate and his craftsmanship faulty; and many works published during the past twenty-five years had rendered the basic premises of *The Heavenly City* invalid.

I think that this is not an unfair summation of the critique of the Moderns—at any rate, I have taken it from their own documentary evidence. It is worthy of note, however, that their presentation was characterized by scholarly objectivity and academic good manners— in fact, it was the very type of precise, analytical evaluation that Becker himself enjoyed so hugely and was wont to indulge in at every opportunity. When they had finished, I for one had received much food for thought. Needless to say, these "revelations," coming as they did from scholars more expert in the fields of thought and science than Becker ever was, left me somewhat shaken. Moreover, it caused me to wonder if what was to follow in the afternoon Reassessment might not turn out to be as overly subjective as the morning Critique had been overly objective.

Happily, my apprehensions anent the performance of the Ancients proved, for the most part, to be pointless, even though it did appear that they tended to concentrate upon a defense of Becker rather than upon a vigorous counterattack against his critics. The members of the panel seemed to regard the basic thesis of *The Heavenly City* as still tenable, and one of them pointed out that if the thesis now seemed trivial it was probably because it had become familiar. They stressed the need for viewing the book in the light of the climate of opinion of its time, in the context of eighteenth-century historiography as of 1932; and they conceded that if Becker were writing the lectures in 1956 his approach would doubtless be quite different from that of twenty-five years ago.

Continuing, the Ancients emphasized the fact that the book was not intended to be a complete picture and that no one should consider it as such. They reminded their hearers that whatever Becker wrote was designed pri-

John Hall Stewart

marily to challenge the readers, to make them think, and, consequently, it should not be accepted too literally. If *The Heavenly City* had been taken rather for what it seemed than for what it actually was, that was less a reflection upon Becker than upon credulous readers who failed to view the work in its proper setting. Incidentally, one of the Ancients suggested that a significant feature of the book was the manner in which it renewed the debate on the place of the *philosophes* in the causes of the French Revolution.

To some extent the defenders admitted agreement with the critics. They were willing to grant that the book did have shortcomings—one of them even went so far as to question its being ranked as a classic because it was not consistently well written. They agreed that the work showed the weakness of a study limited to the field of ideas and that, as a pedagogical device, it should be used with care. But by and large they seemed to feel that the defects were neither so numerous nor so serious as the critics had claimed and that the "attack" was principally the result of misunderstanding. As for the claims of the Moderns that Becker's idea of continuity in comparing the thirteenth and the eighteenth centuries was unsound, they replied (and this was their most telling rejoinder) that *The Heavenly City* was essentially a study in parallels, and not in continuity at all.

In the all-too-brief concluding discussion from the floor, both groups continued their debate, but two comments stood out prominently. One was to the effect that if the book was accepted at face value, there would be little to criticize, whereas if it was not accepted in this

160

manner, the reader would be out of sympathy with it. The other suggested that perhaps the entire discussion resolved itself into the problem of whether Becker was writing history or something else.

As the session terminated, I found myself wondering just what had been accomplished. Had the Moderns said, in effect, "This is a great book, but we do not think it is a *good* one?" Had they implied, "It may possibly have been all right when it was written, but it cannot survive the scrutiny of modern scholarship?" Had they suggested, "Anyway, it is not the type of book that Becker should have written?" Had the Ancients replied, "Whatever its defects, we still think it is essentially a great book *and* a good one?" Had they intimated, "In any case, how could *you* evaluate it, you who were not privileged to know the man or to work with him?" Had they insinuated, "You read too much into it and not enough out of it?"

Had both sides, for some inexplicable reason, overlooked a question which was basic to the entire discussion, namely, "How can anyone ever really know?" The Ancients had argued from their "understanding" of *The Heavenly City*, the Moderns from their "knowledge" of it. Was either group capable of finding the answers which it sought, or had those answers died with the man who provided the questions? Was his benign spirit looking down upon our serious assembly and chuckling at the thought of the controversy he had provoked? Could it be possible (and I had posed this question myself) that Becker, with his Voltairean cast of mind, had been guilty of playing a "pack of tricks," not upon the dead but

John Hall Stewart

upon the living who survived him? Was the net result of the entire discussion reminiscent of nothing more than the case of the blind men and the elephant?

As I endeavored to adjust my perspective of the proceedings, I reverted to my own questions and comments. They no longer seemed adequate as a means of enabling me to state my own position, but they did appear valid as a source of further questions for that purpose. These I finally worded as follows: (1) Why did Becker write *The Heavenly City*, and what was he trying to achieve? (2) Why has the book been so well received for so many years, and why has it met with little serious criticism heretofore? (3) Is there any satisfactory explanation of the "faulty scholarship" which the Moderns seem to have detected in the work? (4) How should we Ancients consider the approach of the Moderns to *The Heavenly City*? (5) In view of the somewhat devastating dissection which the Moderns appear to have performed upon it, does *The Heavenly City* have any future as a serious work of scholarship? In seeking answers to these questions, in the sequence in which they have been presented, I have attempted to resolve my thoughts and afterthoughts on the symposium. I am fully aware that at best such reflections can never be more than opinions and assumptions based upon guesswork and inadequate evidence.

Why did Carl Becker write *The Heavenly City*, and what was he trying to achieve? The incidental reason for writing it was, of course, an invitation from Yale University to deliver a series of lectures. The essential reasons, however, insofar as we can guess at them, would seem to be in the nature of things. Although I cannot

162

substantiate it with documentation (and a historian without evidence is at an obvious disadvantage), I have long felt that a work approximating *The Heavenly City* would have appeared sooner or later, without special external motivation. It seems to me that by 1930 or thereabouts Becker had reached a point in his intellectual development where he wished to attempt something of a synthesis of his thinking during a lifetime of historical study.

In the interval between the publication of *The United States: An Experiment in Democracy* in 1920 (republished with a revised title in 1927) and the appearance of *The Heavenly City* in 1932, Becker wrote a great deal. Only two of his efforts, however, took the form of books —*The Declaration of Independence: A Study in the History of Political Ideas,* in 1922, and a high-school textbook, *Modern History: The Rise of a Democratic, Scientific, and Industrialized Civilization,* in 1931. Both of these works, especially in their subtitles, suggested the direction of Becker's thinking, and it is but logical to assume that he wished to carry it farther. The Yale lectures in a sense only provided a convenient pretext for doing, at a particular time, something that probably was already taking shape in his mind.

Moreover, lectures as such afforded him an acceptable means of expression. Those who knew Becker will doubtless agree that what he had in mind could never have taken the form of a weighty tome, replete with the mechanics of professional historical scholarship. He had done his share of that sort of labor long since, and he no longer had either the time or the patience for such an undertaking. Leave that to others "more learned"; he would be content to distill the results of their labors to achieve what was, to him at least, the real end result. In this instance it was an attempt to show why and how men have thought and acted as they did at different times and in divers places. It was but natural that, in view of his previously demonstrated interest in the thought of eighteenth-century America, he should approach his problem by way of contemporaneous developments in Europe, especially in France, where so many of those developments originated and flourished. (In fact, we were told in the afternoon discussion from the floor that, when he first went to Cornell University, Becker had expressed the hope that one day he might be able to write something about the *philosophes!* [1])

Here it may be well to suggest a possibility which many readers of *The Heavenly City* seem to have overlooked. Interested as he was in historical causation in general and the causes of the French Revolution in particular, it is quite likely that, despite his explicit statement renouncing concern for "consequences" in favor of a consideration of "preconceptions," [2] Becker was directing his examination of eighteenth-century ideas toward their relationship with what happened in 1789. As I recall his approach to the French Revolution, Becker was always more concerned with causes than with events. He was fully aware that the Revolution was a fundamental institutional change which evolved from a society in which there was considerable discontent with the existing order. But he appeared to be unwilling to accept the discontent as sufficient in itself to produce the change that eventually materialized. In his search for other pro-

[1] *Supra*, 135.   [2] *Heavenly City*, 33.

vocative elements in the prerevolutionary era he seemed
to find the real answer for motivation and action in ideas.

Now the evaluation of ideas as causative factors in historical development has always been a difficult task, so
difficult that historians have frequently circumvented
it. To Becker, however, it apparently presented a challenge that must be met, despite the obvious hazards involved in dealing with matters at once intangible and
elusive. I do not know whether he had read Gustave Le
Bon on *The Psychology of Revolution* [3] or Lyford P.
Edwards on *The Natural History of Revolution* [4] or other
works of this type. From what I was able to observe of
his reading tastes and habits, however, I strongly suspect
that he had given considerable attention to this form of
literature and that he had been influenced by it.

Certainly, as he had already made clear in his textbook, he had reached some definite conclusions about
the place of ideas in fomenting a revolution. Ideas
seemed to serve several purposes. They tended to make
thinkers examine the problems of their day more criti-
cally. They afforded a means of "rationalizing" demands
for change. They provided concepts out of which a new
set of institutions might be constructed. What is true of
the textbook is generally true of *The Heavenly City* as
well. For here, too, he was endeavoring to ascertain the
manner in which ideas take form, the way in which they
are received, and the use to which they are put, with
special reference to the prerevolutionary period in Europe. If one were to change the title of the book to *Some
Intellectual Origins of the French Revolution,* the general
impression gained from it would not be altered appre-

[3] New York, 1913. [4] Chicago, 1927.

ciably. (Perhaps such a change might have been desirable in 1932—at least it might have precluded some of the differences of interpretation which appeared in 1956!)

Incidentally, in connection with the origins of *The Heavenly City*, a feature suggested by Ancients and Moderns alike should be noted before proceeding further. This feature is in the nature of a paradox, viz., that, although *The Heavenly City* is doubtless considered by many as the "mature product" of Becker's "peak years," nonetheless, in some respects it was only something of a "trial run." It was certainly something of a transition, for it appears to me to be more representative of the type of writing in which he indulged after 1932 than before that year. To me this paradox is, and doubtless will remain, one of the most interesting features of the work.

Why has the book been so well received for so many years, and why has it met with little serious criticism heretofore? By the time that Becker produced *The Heavenly City*, he had come to enjoy a reputation as a stylist among historians. Hence this volume, the first of several slim "essays" during his later years, had something of an audience already waiting it. Moreover, whatever defects might have been apparent in the literary craftsmanship, for the most part the book did read well and smoothly. It also provided many examples of enchanting "neatly-turned phrases" for which Becker had such a flair. And, by and large, it presented in a provocative and disarmingly simple manner an analysis of men and events that hitherto had been buried in the verbiage of less articulate writers. It was not without

166

good reason, therefore, that *The Heavenly City* met with an enthusiastic response on the part of a relatively wide reading public.

Nor was the audience limited to professors or intellectual laymen of the author's own generation. By the 1930s Becker had a following of admirers (devoted, some of them, to the point of utter subjectivity—these he would have chided good-naturedly had he been aware of their attitude), former graduate students now engaged in teaching in colleges and universities and specializing, for the most part, in some phase of the history of eighteenth-century Europe. It was to be expected that these disciples would rally to the words of the master and would relay them, in turn, to their own students. Sometimes, I fear, too many of these "partisans" read the book much as Becker said the men of the Enlightenment read the works of the Philosophers—their appreciation was more superficial than fundamental; they gave more attention to the wit and cynicism and negations than they did to the serious remarks and affirmations.

Hence I am convinced that much of the uncritical approach to *The Heavenly City* may be attributed to a form of hero worship. I have already mentioned, however, that the book appeared to be a simple, charming statement of complex matters, which any literate person could read with pleasure and understanding, whereas in the past such statements had been denied the "common reader," who was unfamiliar with the specialized vocabularies of philosophers, scientists, mathematicians, and the like. Becker's dangerously simple approach to his problems undoubtedly had something to do with arousing interest in his work and minimizing adverse criticism of it. On the other hand, in leaving the realm of "cold facts" (however "relative" they might be) and entering the area of ideas and science and their inter-relationships (especially with simplifications and generalizations), Becker was, to a degree, leaving himself open to vigorous attack somewhere along the line. That "somewhere" seems at last to have arrived with a newer generation of scholars who are experts in the fields into which he ventured.

Is there any satisfactory explanation of the "faulty scholarship" which the Moderns seem to have detected in *The Heavenly City?* If there is, I think it may be found in an understanding of the man and his approach to his work. Carl Becker was fully aware of the limits of time, energy, and capacity within which the historian is forced to work; and in his associates, Professors Burr and Hull (and I say this with no disrespect intended), he could hardly have failed to observe two shining examples of the danger of scholarly thoroughness carried to an extreme. And (as I have already suggested) having done his share of "definitive research" at the beginning of his career, he apparently had decided that thenceforth he would do the best that he could without resorting further to that enervating form of effort. He would try to get along with the materials that he could use, the ones that seemed most suited to the task at hand.

If Becker failed to exploit certain sources of information, it was undoubtedly because he had no desire to utilize them—he may even have deemed them unnecessary for his purposes. On the other hand, had he attempted to use all of them, it is questionable if his knowledge, especially of science, would have been equal to the task. Unlike his colleague, Preserved Smith (who was probably the exception rather than the rule), Becker was doubtless incapable of approaching the study of Newton by reading a first edition of the *Principia* and then availing himself of the expert counsel of professional mathematicians to clarify the details. For that matter, how many historians, even in this day of fine specialization, would be capable of following such a course? In the last analysis, all of us are hopelessly dependent upon interpretations by others, whether of information that we do not understand or of data that we have no time to verify.

In any case, Becker was concerned primarily with the essential principles of Newton's work, the manner in which they seemed to be received, and the influence that they appeared to exert on the thought of the succeeding generation. This information he could obtain rather from an appreciation and comprehension of generalities than through a proficiency in mathematical or scientific minutiae. Like his friends, the Philosophers, Becker may have felt that he did not have to read the *Principia* in order to understand what it represented. Like them, also, he may easily have been a victim of misunderstanding and delusion; but this can be the fate of any man at any time.

Even in the realm of ideas, where he was dealing basically with knowledge conveyed through the everyday medium of words rather than through the less familiar instrumentality of scientific formulas and mathematical symbols, Becker may have been guilty of too much assumption or too little reading. This, too, can happen to anyone. Even the experts, in their limited

169

fields of investigation, must pick and choose. They cannot possibly know all that needs to be known. And certainly they are not above indulging in hypotheses. I feel sure that Becker was fully conscious of his own limitations. I find it difficult to believe that, relativist that he was, he was unaware of the pitfalls in what he was doing to such an extent that he would not try to avoid some of the more obvious ones.

In the study of ideas, although the statement of the ideas themselves may be quite clear, any absolute determination of their effect upon a wide and varied audience is difficult to achieve with any degree of assurance. Yet we must remember that where the leading thinkers of an age are concerned, one can see in their writings the manner in which they have seized upon whatever was useful to them in the works of a previous era and the way in which they have made it serve their needs. This is precisely what Becker tried to do. If his conclusions seem unwarranted or unorthodox, it should be no source of astonishment to anyone in our profession. Two equally competent, equally learned historians may examine the same body of evidence and yet may produce differing interpretations of it. If this is possible in the case of analyses based upon "facts," is it not more likely to occur when the analyses are founded upon the less tangible material of ideas?

How should we Ancients consider the approach of the Moderns to *The Heavenly City?* As I have already suggested, a "new approach" to Becker, in a spirit adversely critical of *The Heavenly City,* was bound to come sooner or later. I am inclined to feel that if it had not come, some of Becker's skeptical opinions with regard to the future might have been justified. Certainly, were he living, I am sure that he would have derived considerable satisfaction from it. The remarks of the Ancients themselves suggest that perhaps this new approach is only a bolder manifestation of something that has been going on, in a somewhat restrained manner, all the time. And the claims of the Moderns have simply brought it into clearer focus, in a sort of "delayed reaction."

The book does have defects—but what book does not? Up to the present the shortcomings seem to have been overshadowed by the more attractive features. Now, however, the newer generation of specialists has presented numerous specific grounds for criticism; they have pointed up omissions and meanings which have escaped many of the Ancients to date. If there are good grounds for their charges, we must face up to them. The extent to which we accept them as whole cloth, however, depends upon the extent to which the Moderns are willing to re-examine them in the light of necessary qualifying factors, some of which I have attempted to present in the foregoing paragraphs.

Perhaps the Moderns have been unaware of or indifferent to the origin and meaning of *The Heavenly City* in its broader perspective. Perhaps they have been viewing it in a species of "isolation." Perhaps they have failed to see it clearly in the context of its authorship and its climate of opinion. Perhaps they have neglected to recognize that sometimes more than academic learning is necessary in substantiating critical claims. Perhaps they have been remiss in the matter of tempering their erudition with subtlety. Perhaps, as Becker said of the *philosophes*, they have become the victims of their own "common sense," a common sense founded upon pure scholarship alone.

On the whole, however, I feel that we Ancients should welcome their "iconoclasm" in the spirit in which it has been presented. It emanated from no other source than honest critical scholarship, the type, as I have already stressed, which Becker himself would have been the first to approve. It may be a good thing, especially for those who have approached his work in too uncritical a spirit. It may serve as a reminder that times and circumstances change, and with them opinions and values. Above all, it may make us aware of the danger of putting thoughts into print for all to read.

What of the final question? In view of the somewhat devastating dissection which the Moderns appear to have performed upon it, does *The Heavenly City* have any future as a work of serious scholarship? I for one can give no positive answer. Who could have foreseen in 1932 that the little volume would run through ten printings and still be going strong, if only as a target for criticism, twenty-five years later? Who can tell how much longer it will continue to be read, whether for enjoyment, enlightenment, or faultfinding? It is the misfortune of the historian that he cannot predict (at least with any certainty)—otherwise he might revel in the esteem traditionally bestowed upon soothsayers. Unhappily, the historian is tied to the past. Only insofar as that past can provide clues can he even venture suggestions as to the future.

Where books are concerned, however, the historian may safely assume that the passage of time will render most of them outmoded. He may be fairly sure that new researches and new points of view will relegate them to the shelves of "classics," those works which continue to be admired for what they once were but which are no longer used because of what they have become. Yet as he examines these masterpieces of an earlier day, he cannot but be impressed by the fact that they are still considered "classics." However outmoded, be it in form, in substance, or in interpretation, there they remain, historiographical mileposts, evidences of the quality of their time. He must almost be forced to conclude that what is once a classic will always remain one.

It has probably become apparent, long before this concluding paragraph, that I am one of that considerable number of persons who, for one reason or another, and in spite of its obvious defects, consider *The Heavenly City* a classic. It should be no source of surprise to anyone, therefore, if I go so far as to offer two more or less patent conjectures with regard to the future of the book. First, I feel that, if it is a classic, it will continue to be a subject of controversy for some time to come. Second, and for the same reason, I feel that it will continue to be read. I might even risk a third conjecture, to wit, that it will be designated Becker's "great work," long after his others may have been forgotten.

EDWARD WHITING FOX

CORNELL UNIVERSITY

12. Reflections on the Trial of Carl Lotus Becker

IN the preceding pages Carl Becker stands arraigned as being no better a historian than he should have been. Historians assembled for the sad and solemn business of judging a fellow scholar, we could not but be reminded, one would hope with some increase of that sympathetic understanding from which all truly great history derives, of those countless unhappy occasions when honest peers had been called to the stern duty of considering the aberrations of brilliant but wayward colleagues.

The prosecution, as is customary in such affairs, based its case on a single incriminating document: *The Heavenly City of the Eighteenth-Century Philosophers.* Nor was the gravity of the indictment one whit lessened by Mr. Becker's clear disclaimer of any intention, at least in the writing of this essay, of being a historian at all.[1]

[1] Charlotte Watkins Smith, *Carl Becker* (Ithaca, N.Y., 1956), 212.

Reflections on the Trial

Whatever his intentions may have been, *The Heavenly City* has long since come to be recognized not only as history, but what is worse, history that has set a standard of elegant urbanity for an entire generation while insidiously disseminating heretical and offensive views about a great century of our tradition. Fortunately, however, our task is lightened by the knowledge that the accused is quite safe from any consequences of our verdict and that we are probably equally safe from all revenge, save perhaps a distant, disembodied chuckle.

Since all of us know only too well the compromising text, and all the seductions which have made it one of the best-known and best-loved books about the eighteenth century; and since all of us have followed with admiring attention the arguments brought before this court—the masterful accusation of our chief prosecutor, Dr. Peter Gay, and the incisive, dispassionate testimony of so many distinguished witnesses—there is no need to review the entire *procès* of the trial. It will suffice to single out for final reconsideration those major issues on which our verdict will necessarily be based.

The formulation of specific charges, as distinguished from the recognition of obvious general error, proved awkward at the very start. Clearly Mr. Becker made a number of errors of fact, but a judgment based on these slips alone would set a dangerous precedent. Let him amongst us . . . ! Even so, some of the errors were hardly trivial, some were the result of very careless scholarship, or, do we dare say it in front of our students, of practically no scholarship at all. Others would almost seem to have been willfully committed in the interest of mere style. It's hard to know which would be worse, but it is frighteningly easy to wonder if any would have caused Carl Becker a decent twinge of remorse.

It would only be embarrassing to discover how little history of science he had read, if one were not threatened with the revelation that he really didn't care. And yet what else could be expected of a man addicted to turning brilliant phrases without even a glance over his shoulder at the historical consequences they might have in tow. Take, for example, his statement that the *philosophes* "dismantled heaven, somewhat prematurely [it would seem], since they retained their faith in the immortality of the soul." A more disingenuous and devilish bit of libel it would be hard to find; and yet any serious scholar would have known that virtually none of the *philosophes* believed in the *immortality* of the soul.[2] With the imperceptible flicker of Saladin's scimitar, the phrase leaves the unwary reader—like the unlucky slave in the legend—insensible of the fatal stroke. Without benefit of scholarship, one would inevitably assume that Voltaire, Diderot, and all the others regarded themselves as an aspirant heavenly host preparing to sit on the right hand of Reason in the last page of History. We are not, alas, the first members of the clerical tradition to be forced to contemplate the dangers of a too-polished style.

Nor can Professor Gottschalk divert our attention by his brilliant paradox about the bad writing in the compromising text.[3] Filled with careless phrasing and excess verbiage though *The Heavenly City* may seem to be, its lines still glow with the disintegrating charm which has already so damaged the public character of the Age of

[2] *Supra,* 37.   [3] *Supra,* 89.

Reason. If Mr. Becker would not have allowed his students the same literary liberties, he may well have been right. In any case, the anecdote, related by Val Lorwin, of the split infinitive which he so helpfully attempted to repair in one of the master's manuscripts suggests, apparently, that neither would he have expected them to correct his style. He might, in fact, have felt justified in withholding the final secrets of his craft from even his most promising disciples, and the successful use of excess verbiage may never have been included in his syllabus of instruction.

Damaging as these preliminary charges are, they will not carry the burden of the case. Even if we could demonstrate that Mr. Becker preferred following the fool's gold of fine phrases to honest digging in the established mines of documents, we should not have pressed our charges very far. The jury might be swayed, or at least prepared, if we could say: "Gentlemen, a historian capable of ignoring relevant materials, of writing too well with deliberate intent, is a man capable of slander against the noblest of centuries." But afterward we should be left facing our own rules of evidence and be forced to admit that all of this had not proved much.

The real issue, as Professor Gay insists, is not these tangible mistakes but the fact that Carl Becker unerringly posed the central question for historians of the eighteenth century: the question of persistence and change, and then consistently provided the wrong answer. *The Heavenly City* begins, as Mr. Gay reminds us, with the doubtful dialogue between Aquinas and Voltaire designed to show that apparent persistence can conceal important change and that even dramatic changes can be no more than new clothes for old continuities. If we cannot but agree with Dr. Gay that this is indeed the "right question," we can hardly fail to admit that Mr. Becker handled it with scant respect.

Elusive as he always was in matters of professional faith, Mr. Becker clearly treated the dogma of Change with something less than reverence in the pages of this essay. After that treacherously candid opening in which he dramatized the change in the concept of reason since St. Thomas' day he slyly deflates—as Mr. Gay has been at considerable trouble to demonstrate—the significance of the big changes which undeniably took place in the early eighteenth century, leaving nothing standing but the persistence of human fallibility. This was, of course, the sort of witty paradox the *philosophes* themselves had so brilliantly employed. Just so long as men had clung to the heresy of revelation, it was useful as well as diverting to insist that no amount of superficial change could touch the deep persisting error of credulity. Only after the chorus of Voltaire and Locke, Hume and Rousseau, had shouted hosannas to Nature and decreed Light to men did the educated and enlightened recognize that a decisive and irreversible change had taken place. Almost everything important still remained to be learned; but finally men could see the way, develop the methods, and work the materials of experience so that eventually, even in a court such as this, it would be possible to say with gratifying conviction, and appropriate reference to the sources: "Here is the Truth."

Hard as it is to comprehend, Carl Lotus Becker seems to have remained smilingly skeptical in the presence of even this form of Incarnation which has become the central article of our faith. An outright defiance would have been less blasphemous. Becker, the distinguished historian—whether he denied it or not—the twentieth-century *philosophe* whose own Heavenly City one would have supposed to be that very Age of Reason he surveyed with such ironic tolerance, this prince of our profession, invariably found persistence where manifestly there was change. Grave as the offense was, and in spite of the fact that our accused appears to accept the charge without excuse, remorse, or even real concern, we cannot allow the accusation to be transformed into a final judgment by default. If we are to do our duty with the diligence befitting our profession, we must provide our defendant with the best counsel that can be found. Nor for that matter is there any lack of witnesses for his case. More than most professors of history, Carl Becker was loved and revered by his students. No word against his memory will go unchallenged if one of his disciples is at hand; and no matter what the critical word may have been, the character of the defense seems usually to be the same.

Carl Becker, the faithful tend to say—Carl Becker of all people—cannot be understood merely from his published works. To read him accurately and fully, they maintain, it is necessary to have sat at his feet, and yet the inability to transfer to paper the heady elixir of the lesson well taught, which is too often the last infirmity of the inspiring teacher, would hardly seem to fit Carl Becker. More than anything else, Mrs. Smith in her excellent study has made it possible for us to follow the care with which he chose his words, the skill with which he ordered them, and the endless, loving impatience with which he worked and reworked his phrases, until with the final touches, the freshly split infinitive here, the fastidiously selected excess verbiage there, the whole page comes to life with the artful rusticity of plain old Ben Franklin, beneath whose simple coat beat a warmer and more sophisticated heart than could be found on many a courtly sleeve he might have rubbed during his triumphal progress at Versailles. No, if Mr. Becker taught for his students, he wrote for us, all of us, and we shall have to demand our fair equality of opportunity to peruse the text and make of it what we may without the interference of inspired exegesis.

And so once again we find ourselves facing the bewitching pages of *The Heavenly City,* bearing witness to the author's baffling insistence on finding continuity where manifestly there was change—change in science, in the governance of states, in commerce, in society, and above all in the standards of truth which happily were finally brought to a useful stage. Becker does not, of course, go so far as to deny the obvious fact of change; he simply fails to be adequately impressed. Nor are the dangers of this cunning skepticism allowed to escape unnoticed, for Mr. Gay has reminded us that even though *The Heavenly City* was once approved by the liberals, it has now become, and by no mere accident, a favorite of the New Conservatives, a charge that might be expected to have ruffled even Mr. Becker's equanimity if it were not remembered how gently, if sadly, he suffered the liberals of yesteryear.

The main question before us, and we must not allow ourselves to be distracted by even such intriguing irrelevancies as the New Conservatism, the main question is Change. It should hardly be necessary in this company to insist further upon the significance of Change. Surely each of us must realize that without Change there would be no History, only Philosophy hopelessly floundering in a morass of social science. Since such an alternative is not to be contemplated, we need waste no more time in affirming our faith in Change.

To make this affirmation, however, is not necessarily to insist on the infallibility of all its prophets among the *philosophes*. It is hardly now a secret that they were at times in error, that on occasion even the best of them would hold with unreasonable tenacity to a belief that was all too soon to reveal a fatal weakness. If Mr. Becker were a less slippery adversary, we should want to admit that these disturbing lapses of philosophic virtue do point to the persistence of weakness in even the best of mortals, but to grant him this point would give him an opening to lead the case astray. That Voltaire may have been a touch naïve about the power of reason or Locke a bit superficial in his analysis of the human mind is not quite the same as to infer that Voltaire's reason was no more than Aquinas' faith, that Locke's total innocence of the newborn mind was no more than the silver lining of Christianity's dark doctrine of the total depravity of the soul turned inside out.

It is this sort of implied paradox that is most damaging and most perplexing. The whole concept is preposterous, and no one more than Mr. Becker, latter-day *philosophe* that he was, should have known better. In a hearty after-dinner speech this little *jeu de mots* might have had its place, but here, respectably clothed in the pages of a book, presented with only the slightest smile, it inevitably becomes a much graver matter.

Mr. Becker, who hated bigotries as much as Voltaire,

knew as well as we that Reason alone had mastered the fanaticism of religious faith and that only Reason and its systematic development in Science offered hope of progress toward the solid salvation of a rational new and better world. In fact, if our accused had not so many and so determined witnesses to his character, if he were not so firmly established as "one of the goodly company . . . who wished mankind well," it would almost seem that he had devoted his life to creating problems in intellectual history, not to solving them.

Take, for example, the verbal game he played in asserting that both the thirteenth and eighteenth were centuries of faith. In the former, "faith" put the accepted answers to the big questions beyond the reach of rational criticism; in the latter, "reason" examined all those questions by a method so clearly superior to revelation, authority, or tradition that it inevitably commanded a new and total confidence. What point, we are forced to ask, could Mr. Becker have found in calling this confidence by the compromising name of "faith" unless he wanted to undermine the very foundations of our hard-won Truth. It is this evasive failure to distinguish unequivocally between the claims of revelation and science that so seriously incriminates his whole attitude toward historical persistence.

To equate, as he did, the theory of a beautifully articulated world machine with the Biblical myth of the creation of the world, or to try to reproduce a doctrine of the Fall of Man by comparing eighteenth-century nostalgia for the golden age of Rome or the Arcadian civilization of Pennsylvania with the medieval belief in an obviously fictitious Eden, was willfully to trifle with the

standards of our profession. Obviously the utopias of the
philosophes were constructed to establish worldly standards by which to judge and condemn the iniquities of
their age. Obviously any similarity between this and the
role of Eden in Christian teaching must have been wholly
coincidental. This skillfully contrived confusion can be
reduced, as Mr. Gay points out, to an equation of the
philosophe's frank recognition of the absolute value of
his objective Truth with the mystical "certainties" of the
Christian bigot. Such a conclusion would seem to put Mr.
Becker in a position of objecting to certainty, the very
concept of Truth itself, rather than to the specific and
infamous "certainties" of the medieval Church. Could it
be that he had missed the whole point of the Enlightenment, that he did not realize it was the malign errors of
Christian "truth," but not Truth, as such, that was under
attack?

It is perhaps a question that should be pondered carefully. After all, we do know that Mr. Becker worked and
reworked, over a long period of time, his views on the
nature of historical fact. He began promisingly enough
by cutting away much of the dross of contemporaneous
historical theory and practice, demonstrating effectively
with what care and precision facts had to be pared and
polished. But instead of stopping with a job well done,
he continued the process until the "fact" disappeared
before our very eyes. A spectacular bit of faking to be
sure, but one that was downright irresponsible in a member of our profession!

Clearly a historian who would trifle this lightheartedly
with facts would not be a man to trust with Truth or
Change, and yet this line of speculation would bring us,

sooner or later, to the brink of a terrible discovery. Could it be that Mr. Becker was not merely a careless historian but that he was, if one dares say it, the Anti-Historian himself? Such a charge would have to be formulated with care since it would run the double risk of making a martyr of our accused and exposing us to the charge of having inflated the significance of a simple case out of vulgar self-importance. But once stated, the idea is hard to dispel.

Inevitably we recall the passage in *The Heavenly City* about the Enlightenment historians in which Mr. Becker describes with kindly condescension their departure "under the banner of objectivity and with a flourish of scholarly trumpets" and their failure "to pass the boundaries of the eighteenth century." [4] It is precisely this sort of *léger-de-plume* that makes the man so dangerous; one can hardly tax him directly with misunderstanding, or downright misrepresentation, of the facts without having him seem to say, with that disquieting air of innocence, "But really, my friend, these monsters which you encounter in my pages are nothing but some toy windmills I've been making for my own amusement. And what do you call your horse, Rocinante? He does look a bit thin and tired; may I offer him a lump of sugar?"

Well, we're in it now, and there's no turning back. Carl Becker was wrong about the eighteenth century. He was wrong about the Enlightenment historians. They wrote excellent history, and whatever boundaries they crossed they did carry the banner of objectivity and paid a lot more attention to their sources and the accuracy of their statements than Mr. Becker did.

[4] *Supra,* 47.

Moreover, they understood the use of History. They realized fully that it recorded the path of humanity in its progress from ignorance to knowledge, from superstition to science, that its basic subject was fundamental Change, not superficial persistence. They believed, with a confidence derived from their scrupulous use of Reason, that History not only illuminated the path of progress in the past, but as clearly indicated what it would be in the future. In spite of all the brilliance and resourcefulness of their rational analysis of society and of their ability to identify existing Evil and to formulate measures for its extirpation—in spite of all, they depended on History to demonstrate their theses, to encourage their followers, and, where necessary, to bring their enemies to submission by the threat of condemning them to eternal damnation in the pages of humanity's proud record. Well, there it is: History embodied the Truth achieved by Change, and it was only from the doctrine of this trinity that the gospel of social progress was derived. Perhaps Mr. Becker would like to see himself in the pages of History not only as an indifferent historian, but as an Anti-Historian and a discovered enemy of social progress?

In all honesty it is difficult not to wonder if he would have cared. And yet we know that in the great crisis of the Nazi challenge he enlisted in "the goodly company." He wasn't, it is true, much good at marching and seldom kept in step, but once the great battle had been clearly joined he fought the good fight and with telling effect. But why, one is compelled to wonder, why couldn't he have seen the issue sooner? Some of the rest of us, it is true, also made serious errors in those years; some even started down the path of isolation; but if our answers

185

were wrong, only for the moment of course, they were at least the product of scrupulous research and, once arrived at, were held with respectable conviction.

Mr. Becker, one would gather from his attitude, had not really consulted history as a guide for action at all. In fact, he gave the impression of believing that history taught nothing so much as that history taught nothing with useful certainty and, on these grounds, appeared to take it as a guide to inaction instead. Perhaps that is why the content, as distinguished from the philosophy, always seemed to bore him so. But—with Carl Becker as with Zadig there was always one more "but"—but then why did he write history at all? Mrs. Smith would seem to say: "to write," rather than "for history." But to write about what?

Could it be that all his intriguing and elegant essays were only introspection: "There but by the grace of History go I, Carl Becker, no better, if no worse, than if I'd fallen into a different age"? Were these little forays that crossed no boundaries and winded their curious paths without benefit of banners or trumpets merely our old colleague making his way up the stairs of his imagination to try on once again those fancy but faded costumes he found in the attic of the Past? One thinks of Machiavelli whiling away the long nights of exile in his toga, but then Machiavelli was so much better a historian, and, for that matter, so much more serious and responsible a citizen.

Machiavelli knew that only in reading the past could he solve the problems of the future. He did, unfortunately, allow himself to be carried away here and there by his enthusiasms (with results that should warn us all to maintain a decent outward objectivity), but at least he fought the good fight without a guilty, embarrassed air. With Becker it was as though he were ashamed of being in the right. When suddenly confronted with the Truth, he could appear almost as frightened as if he'd seen a ghost; and student of the Enlightenment that he was, he knew perfectly well that ghosts don't exist.

To fear Truth, even to hate Truth, is nothing new. The bigots, the selfish men with vested interests in corrupt societies, and all the rest of their doleful crew have hated and feared and fought the Truth throughout the pages of our books. But Carl Becker wished mankind well, he hated bigotries, distrusted vested interests, exposed old errors—even if he did tend to see them as human foibles rather than monstrous crimes—and lived a blameless, almost exemplary, life, except for this strange, elusive levity, this shimmering phosphorescence of his boredom caught in the crystal mirror of his prose.

Enchantingly innocuous as all this may seem, and there's no denying the attractive quality of *The Heavenly City*, its impact is, in final analysis, downright perverse. Tolerance of human weakness has always been accounted a private virtue; but it is not the sort of doctrine that should be elevated to public use, and to balance it with a morbid intolerance of Virtue is perilously close to taking sides, the wrong side, in the struggle between Right and Wrong. And yet in spite of this annoying attitude, Mr. Becker did make the right decision when events finally backed him into a corner where further escape from choice was quite cut off.

Well, there would seem to be more things in this sad and baffling case than most of us, historians, had ever dreamed of: a good man who would make the Good

187

appear no better than it should have been, a historian who emphasized persistence at the expense of Change, a *philosophe* apparently more concerned with the minor errors of his fellow *philosophes* than with all but the greatest evils of *l'infâme*. Not that he liked the forces of Evil; yet most of the time he seemed inclined to accept them as one more element of man's doubtful fate, while the forces of Good clearly caused him apprehension. He was tolerant of his Enlightened friends, amused by their brave blasphemies "of hanging the last king in the entrails of the last priest," but somehow he made them seem so young and overeager. Was Mr. Becker never young? Did he experience no brave blasphemies in his own youth? Did he never even dream of tarring the last social reformer with the whiskers of the last Bible-belt evangelist? Couldn't he realize that History, like Heaven, helps only those who help themselves? This is a scripture so well known that even the devils quote it now: and Khrushchev belches forth a defiant "History is with us" at the West, a statement which might remind us that we have more important work to do. When history gets into hands like those, it is no time for members of this profession to let themselves be distracted by theological refinements. Our duty is clear and our cause is just.

But the disposition of Mr. Becker's case? Perhaps the whole thing was rather a mistake, and the best solution might easily be to leave him to History—keeping in mind the wise Latin tag, already cited by Mr. Gay, which runs: "The fate of books [and those who write them?] depends upon the capacity of the reader."

LEO GERSHOY

NEW YORK UNIVERSITY

13. *The Heavenly City*
of Carl Becker

OF all of Carl Becker's writings, *The Heavenly City of the Eighteenth-Century Philosophers,* if the number of printings is any criterion, is the most admired. Composed rapidly, between the late fall of 1930 and the spring of 1931, it was easily written because the subject matter of those lectures had been in the forefront of his thinking for many years. On a stylistic level, it is Becker at his most delightful, maintaining an easy legato, wearing his learning gracefully and unobtrusively, witty and charmingly urbane. Yet, for all their beguiling literary attractiveness these lectures derived their importance from the thesis that they advance. In them Becker posited and elaborated a heterodox view. The debt of the *philosophes* to their thirteenth-century predecessors, he contended, was greater than they were aware of. Despite great differences between eighteenth-century and thirteenth-century modes of thought, there were also many significant similarities. The *philosophes* were less emancipated from the preconceptions of medieval thought than they realized themselves and than we had supposed; in fact, "making allowances for certain important alterations in the bias," their preconceptions were essentially the same as those of the thirteenth century. That similarity went far to explain how, as they demolished the Heavenly City of Thomas Aquinas, they rebuilt it with more up-to-date material.

This startling thesis, engrossing to most readers, he placed in a broader philosophical frame of reference. He maintained that each cultural period had its own distinctive quality, its own set of criticized and more often uncriticized generalizations into which entered, on one level or another of consciousness, the hopes, grievances, inhibitions, and aspirations of the age. This quality or mood, he called, borrowing the phrase from Whitehead, who had already borrowed it from another, "the climate of opinion." In Becker's considered judgment there were notably similar moods or assumptions in the two historical climates of opinion which seemed so utterly different.

As he elaborated his ideas, Becker suggested, rather than expounded in detail, that he, too, knew that the answers which the Enlightenment gave to that "phase of 18 century thought" [1] which interested him differed radically from those put forth earlier. The phase he chose to consider revolved around man's fate and the nature

---

[1] "I don't think it likely," he wrote the author in an undated letter late in 1930, "that I shall leave Ithaca . . . until next May [*sic*]. I have consented to give the Storrs Lectures in the Yale Law School in May—four lectures on some phase of 18 century thought."

of the universe. We may assume that he was aware of the gap between the other-worldly perspective of Thomas Aquinas and the mundane eighteenth-century conviction which affirmed that man's unsolved problems were soon, that is relatively soon, to be solved on earth. But he was not writing his book to repeat for all what no one disputed, for example, the disparity between the medieval view of nature as a logical concept and the later picture of nature as a neat machine with its own built-in regulator. Almost parenthetically, as though he found it unnecessary to say what everybody knew, he alluded to the difference between the Thomistic view of natural law as a construction of deductive logic and the later doctrine of natural law as the observed harmonious behavior of material things. He chose, deliberately, not to make too much of those differences. His interest lay elsewhere, in the similarities rather than the differences between Christian ethic and cosmology and "the religion of humanity."

What he chose to examine at close range was, first, the fundamental assumptions underlying the different conclusions. In his judgment those assumptions were the same. In both instances, he reminded his listeners, the preconceptions concerning the nature of man and his existence were similar: life was not empty but meaningful; the drama of man's fate was of paramount significance. According to the theologians, man's primitive innocence had been debased into original sin; if the *philosophes* were to be followed, his natural goodness had been vitiated by unnatural custom. Both outlooks postulated the existence of forces or a power greater than man, a God—however differently conceived and called

—and both felt a sense of obligation to explain His ways to man. Christianity and *philosophie* were also at one in their common assumption that the dignity of the human person commanded respect; both attributed to man certain natural rights and assigned to the proper authorities the role and the duty of protecting him in the exercise of those rights. Possessed of free will and endowed with responsibility for his action, man could satisfactorily work out his destiny. With either interpretation of the cosmic plan before him as an indispensable reference work, he could adjust thought and deed to the providential scheme and improve his lot.

It was not only the similarity of those preconceptions, which he himself could no longer accept, to which Becker called attention. He gave concrete illustrations of the similarity in the thinking processes which had enabled the two groups of thinkers to accept as valid the preconceptions from which their conclusions followed. In both centuries an awkward dilemma had arisen to confront the thinkers as they began to formulate their views, the inescapable necessity of determining whether man was in fact living in a universe governed by a beneficent mind or in a world ruled by indifferent force. And on both occasions the accredited spokesmen, without intent to deceive of course, indulged in some coercing of reason to have it solve the dilemma to their satisfaction and proclaim that the will of God or the law of the Supreme Being governed the world. They made reason amenable by different devices, such as explaining that things were not what they actually seemed, by insisting that only co-operative facts need apply to answer awkward questions, or by reaffirming that after all the heart did have its reasons. Whether one expedient was employed or another, or a more subtle combination of them, by their deftly guided thinking process they formulated cosmologies which enabled man, sophisticated yet believing man, to live comfortably with himself, while expecting still greater happiness at some future date and place, not precisely specified.

Such, in brief compass, is the theme of *The Heavenly City*, the validity of which several able scholars have subjected to searching re-examination. It transpires from the papers presented at the Sixth Annual Meeting of the New York State Association of European Historians, as well as from the discussion from the floor, that many scholars of the Enlightenment had long, if silently, entertained serious reservations. These reservations ranged from criticism of Becker's style to strictures more or less guarded concerning his scholarship and his seemingly unchallenged status as thinker. In the opinion of one commentator, the ten printings of *The Heavenly City* constituted "an unwarranted success."

The voicing of these evaluations has shaken the equanimity of Becker's faithful admirers, probably more than it would have upset Becker himself. Searching questions concerning the substance of his book would have greatly interested him but without unduly disturbing him. So far as his style was concerned, it is no secret that he recognized with some acuteness the difficulty that a writer experienced in conveying his thoughts through words, a difficulty, he was aware, not peculiar to himself. His comment on the immediate reception of his presidential address to the American Historical Association of the same year (1931) suggests the response he might have made had *The Heavenly City* been criticized in his lifetime as it was twenty-five years later. "Many historians," he wrote, "won't think much of this address ["Everyman His Own Historian"]. F. J. Turner was much pleased with it. C. A. Beard and Jameson and Burr also. Of course it isn't up to what I had in mind. But that's an old story." [2]

The criticism, which is expounded in detail in several essays of this symposium, runs somewhat as follows: *The Heavenly City* was deliberately provocative, designed through a willful paradox to stimulate listeners and even shock them. With his customary witty and charming style, playing gaily with words, Becker covered his impatience with his intellectual forebears and veiled a deadly intent to "debunk" the Enlightenment. He wished to reveal the naïveté of the *philosophes,* if not also to expose their fraudulence. On a professional level, the critique continues, it would be seen and should be said that Becker showed unsuspected defects as a historian, displaying an ignorance of some facts that he ought to have known and misinterpreting others that everyone knew. In consequence of his failure to grasp what the *philosophes* were trying to do, in the course of trying to prove that they were unwittingly and unwillingly Christians at their most unchristian moment, he ignored the immense differences which set the two centuries apart and so exaggerated the continuity between the thirteenth century and the eighteenth as to give a totally misleading picture of the Enlightenment. In short, *The Heavenly City* had all the virtues save one, that of being right.

[2] From a letter to the writer, undated, but immediately following the meeting.

The Heavenly City *of Carl Becker*

The trouble arose, the commentaries go on, because Becker disregarded his own warning not to take the term "Heavenly City" too literally. He did not pay enough heed to his own explanation when he said that the *philosophes* dismantled the Heavenly City of Thomas Aquinas only to rebuild it with more up-to-date materials, that he was only maintaining that the dream of infinite progress of mankind and the attainment of human perfection on earth were Utopian illusions. He fell into a trap of his own making when, first, he took his paradox far more seriously than he should have and, second, did so without seeming to be aware of what he was doing. *The Heavenly City* exposed Becker's feet of clay as a historian, or one foot at least. It showed him up as an innocent, almost ludicrously falling into a trap that he had set for other innocents.

The charges are impressive. What is one to make of them? Certainly, one can appreciate the irritation of professional historians over the spectacle of a distinguished fellow craftsman casting a kind of spell over his readers and persuading them to accept as a comprehensive explanation his highly refracted picture of the eighteenth century. No doubt, also, by his paradoxical insistence upon similarities, he made readers all but forget about the differences. Of course, Preserved Smith and Kingsley Martin were available in English to remind readers of the differences, even if for many years Hazard and Cassirer had still to be read in the original. The historians who point out that Becker was not as familiar with the scientific movement of the Enlightenment as he might have been are certainly right. One wonders, however, how much that scholarly *lapsus* seriously impaired his understanding that such scientific knowledge as the eighteenth century did possess had developed from cumulative efforts and that its belief in progress, at least on a conscious level of thought, was an empirically attained conclusion.

Neither sound, believing Christians nor philosophical skeptics, to employ Hume's ironic juxtaposition as Becker did, are entirely happy over the way in which the latter coupled the modes of thought of the two centuries. Blurring patent dissimilarities and deliberately identifying Thomas' God with Voltaire's Supreme Being, Christian "grace" with philosophical "virtue," and "immortality" with "posterity," was audacious but somewhat less than appealing to men whose strong convictions such intellectual badinage affronted. Conversely, to men of sanguine temperament, less concerned over the dilemmas of philosophy than edified by its consolations, his reminders of the failure of the age to explain the existence of evil in a universe governed in harmony with the laws of nature partook not of irony but of unwarranted, even unnecessary, morbidity.

What the critics overlook was that the conclusions he had reached gave Becker himself slight comfort. The awareness that faith and sentiment had come to the rescue of right reason in the Age of the Enlightenment only superficially gave the impression of affording him ironic amusement. *The Heavenly City*, for all its flashes of wit, was somber not insouciant, not playful but grim. The humor was wry with a clear intimation that the last laugh was on man, on Becker, himself. Like the students whom he had been instructing for many years, he presumably knew that the Enlightenment was both the historical culmination of preceding challenges to Christianity and the point of departure for the credo and the hopes of the two centuries which followed. But the course of human events in those centuries, particularly at the moment that he was writing, had belied hope, and not least the hope that he himself had once entertained. Like many another thinker, Becker was convinced in 1931 that the perfectibility of man and the progress of the human race was the Great Illusion of modern times. The "religion of humanity" was as little—or as much—tenable as the orthodox Christianity which it had supplanted. It was high time, he was suggesting, that one took a close look at the origins of that illusion.

No one could have been more personally sympathetic than Becker to the aspirations of the followers of the *philosophes;* no one more impersonally convinced that they were never to be realized. He had rejected Christian theology while still a young man. The acids of modernity had destroyed whatever faith he may once have had that human destiny was entrusted to the care of a deity. Science had eliminated the fixed points established by traditional religion and metaphysics to enable man to distinguish between good and evil. But his confidence was also eroded that reason would flood the world with the light of understanding. Here was the crux of his difficulty.

Far from sharing the generous trust that Dewey placed in the capacity of man to be educated, he was dejected by the monumental and seemingly inexhaustible store of human stupidity and cruelty. Like the satirical novelists and publicists of the twenties, he was disheartened and depressed by the intellectual vulgarity of prosperous

American democracy, the power drives, complacency, and smugness of the successful, the meanness, envy, and small-mindedness of the masses. As a historian he had not failed to note the widening gap between the ideal of democracy and the nineteenth-century reality. When the great depression fell like a blight upon the lives of his contemporaries, he looked with sadness and with bitterness on the waste land around him and the trail of misery in the wake of prosperity. He could not view with equanimity the gathering of the forces of totalitarianism abroad or, at home, rest unmoved by the spectacle of hungry and angry and bewildered men responding to appeals to their passions and their fears.

Where in all these manifestations of man's weaknesses was the guiding creative force of reason! Did not the plight of mankind, leaders playing cynically upon men's emotions and followers responding on a primitive level of fears and taboos, give confirmation to Becker's profound beliefs concerning the subjective nature of men's thinking and its purposive and selective character? Was it not evident, as he maintained, that ideas came to the surface of consciousness only for the sake of behavior? Whether he derived that conviction from Dewey or James or from others does not matter. Like Sterne, but without whimsey, Becker also believed that "millions of thoughts are every day swimming in the thin juice of a man's understanding without being carried backwards or forwards till some little gust of passion or interest drives them to one side."

"For good men and bad, ignorant and enlightened," he wrote, "reason and aspiration and emotion—what we call principles, faith, ideals—are without their knowing it, at the service of complex and subtle instinctive reactions and impulses." [3] What was true of the thinking process in general was also specifically true of the thinking process of historians. History, like philosophy, also reflected and dealt with the presuppositions, frustrations, and hopes of its time. Try as he would, the historian could not escape the impress of his epoch. Its assumptions in the main were his assumptions; its frame of reference was his, regarding time and space, man and nature, life on earth and the hereafter. Its values tended to be his values; its truths, his truths.

Becker was writing *The Heavenly City* in 1931, the same year that he composed and delivered his famous address, "Everyman His Own Historian." In that resounding manifesto of historical relativism he put forth in its most polished and perfected form the philosophy of history that he had been developing from 1910 on, when he first expressed his views in an essay, "Detachment and the Writing of History." And in *The Heavenly City* he was using the Enlightenment as a case study, a specific illustration of his broader theoretical arguments. He also utilized the opportunity of discussing the *philosophes* to intimate that he had as little confidence in the reform projects currently propounded by the twentieth-century descendants of the *philosophes* as he had in the proposals of the earlier apostles of reason.

History, he maintained in "Everyman," was not and could not be actuality. History was written history, and written history was affirmation, a foreshortened and incomplete representation of a reality that once was. To represent all the evidence that ever occurred was clearly

[3] From a letter to William Dodd in 1920, cited in C. W. Smith, *Carl Becker* (Ithaca, N.Y., 1956), 175.

impossible, for the historian of necessity had to work with traces. Assuming it were possible to have all the facts, it would still not be desirable. The worth of history as affirmation of a vanished reality consisted, if it possessed any worth at all, precisely in the selectivity exercised by the researcher and the writer. To carry on research without knowing what one was looking for was a waste of the researcher's time; and the published findings of an effort so conceived would be an abuse of the reader's confidence.

The honest researcher prided himself naturally on coming into the court of history with clean hands. It was only his hands and the notepaper they carried which were clean. Whether he knew it or not, his mind and his heart were already smudged. They bore the impress of ideas and emotions—principles if one approved of them, otherwise prejudices—that he had somehow already acquired. Whether the historian knew it or not, it was those ideas and emotions which overwhelmingly inclined him to make the selections of past evidence that he did. It was not a case of his sticking to the facts; it was a case of the facts sticking to him.

Since history was an inside job, an affair of the mind and heart, "historical facts," not vanished realities, were the data with which the historian worked. Those facts, continued Becker, were of course the best possible affirmation of the reality that professional honesty and expert scientific training could give. Nevertheless, they had the defects of their qualities. They were still not the real thing. They were only records of the real thing that had happened once, like Caesar's crossing of the Rubicon or Booth's shooting of Lincoln. With those records, some lengthy, some brief, and all necessarily if unwittingly refracted, since the observer was part of the observed, the historian worked. For all his conscious detachment the historian too was part of the observed in his procedure of examining reality through the historical facts. In selecting some and excluding others he was guided by his likes and dislikes, by his standards and values. So the historical facts did not speak for themselves. He spoke for them; and through them he expressed what he held to be the truth. Hence the facts were always relatively true, relative to the times and the emotional and philosophical needs of the age. "O History," Becker apostrophized the Muse, "how many truths have been committed in thy name."

The self-evident truths of the eighteenth century were then of a piece with those of the thirteenth; those of the twentieth, with those of the eighteenth. All were variations upon an architectonic model of deception, all illustrations of the persistent and deep desire of men to find a unitary pattern in historical developments, to devise a single mold into which all the facts could be fitted. All those explanations of what had been before and would be again were essentially deterministic, grounded on the premise that history obeyed laws. In consequence all appealed to history, bidding it offer salvation and justice to men and prove to humanity that there was to be a happy ending to present discontent or misery.

For Becker such belief was illusion. It was in the nature of life not to fulfill hopes, of revolutions to be betrayed. After the *philosophes,* there was the French Revolution; after the Marxists, totalitarian Russia. Thinking man, if he were truly wise, would renounce hope. To free himself from the tensions that hope engendered was to escape disappointment, to save himself, if worst came to worst, from the agony of despair. If he followed that counsel, life could not hurt him. Most fittingly Becker ended *The Heavenly City* with a quotation from Marcus Aurelius: "The man of forty years, if he have a grain of sense, in view of this sameness, has seen all that has been and shall be."

To many young readers of the 1930s and 1940s, who had been raised on a rich diet of ironic or cynical explanations of the human scene, his bleak conclusions carried powerful appeal. At the same time those some years older, and of course wiser, felt curiously let down, several of them breaking into print to protest the spectacle of one of America's most thoughtful and admired historians letting his contemporaries down in the great crisis, and either callously or unwittingly refusing to place his uncontested understanding and immense prestige behind the intense yearning of bewildered and unhappy men to enjoy the consolations of history.

Becker himself was far from happy over the conclusions he had then reached. But for several years more he repeated them in his writing, even raising the query in despondent essays whether liberalism after all was not only another way station along the road that humanity had traversed, whether democracy had not played out its role. After plumbing the depths, he was ultimately to regain his buoyancy and reaffirm the credo that his rigorous intellectualism had all but crushed. However, before he could persuade others to believe in those essential values of life in which instinctively and almost reverently he placed his trust, he had first to get out of the dead end to which his thinking had led him. He could not feel justified in trying to bring "spiritual first aid" to humanity, as he wryly reproached others for attempting to do, until he resolved the paradox of holding that truth exists to be searched for while at the same time asserting that man could attain no more than relative truth. His task, because its emotional implications made it more difficult than a retrospective formulation suggests, was to bring opposites together into a co-ordinated whole. He had to square the conviction that the earth would grow cold and "all the imperishable monuments of man will be as if they had never been" with faith in man.

He had to bring together the view that man was no more than a chance deposit on earth and that "science offered only anesthesia in this life and annihilation in the next" with his predisposition to like people who "went on behaving as if human ideals mattered." He had to reconcile his denial of the possibility of attaining absolute truth with his feeling that the distinction between truth and error nevertheless was useful, that the relative truths which the mind of man could attain were still relative to some unknowable but greater reality than their particular needs or desire, truths hence worth living and dying for.[4]

Becker solved his problem in the one way left him. To remain confidently and innocently wrong with Condorcet and Madame Roland, he could not. He would not, being Becker, make a tragic display of his pain and cry out, with Pascal, that the eternal silence of the infinite spaces terrified him. Nor had he any inclination to accept

[4] For the quotations from Becker and the general discussion of that problem, I am indebted to the excellent treatment in C. W. Smith, *op. cit.*, 32–36, 121–125.

Hume's tart suggestion for philosophical skeptics and "fly back to revealed truth with the greatest avidity." Terrified, he was not; believe in revealed truths, he did not. What he could and did do was to join together the two halves of his personality which had never before fitted exactly and put into a single whole the half that was the child of the generous humanitarian Diderot and the other half that was the pupil of the tough-minded Hume.

The Diderot in him wished to be of service to mankind. To serve was to act. But to act one needed belief in what he was doing. Otherwise the will was paralyzed and one carried on a shadowy existence on the most dreary of levels, on the persuasion that effort was futile and achievement empty. So Becker had first to reassert his belief that life in spite of everything was meaningful and man's fate, while tragic, still significant. It was man's destiny, he said, to be crushed by a universe which was unconscious of what he was doing here and offered him only annihilation in the future. Yet insignificant as man was, he alone and no other creature was aware of it. No one else, too, knew what he knew, that the conception of a universe of infinite spaces which crushed him was his creation, "his most ingenious invention, his supreme work of art." If man was weak because he stood alone, he was also most strong when he stood alone, if for no other reason than that there was no other way for him to stand or act. And act, he had to.

The Hume in him, once the hurdle of the problem in epistemology was cleared, forced him to re-examine more closely what it was he held significant and of value in the

meaningful existence of man. He had to define or perhaps redefine what men like himself had to live for. Here,
too, Becker found he could go about his business only by
an act of the will. Choosing to believe had to be a pre-
condition of thinking about whatever it was he believed.
Having over the course of many years examined and rejected in turn all other social ideologies, he reaffirmed
his faith in democracy. Democracy, he knew, did not
conform too closely in its earthly form to the ideal pattern laid up in heaven. At least it was an illusion close to
the heart's desire, more just than any other he knew, more
likely than any other to give expression to the dignity
and worth of man.

Thus Becker discovered that he too, like the *philosophes,* had no alternative but to reconcile diverse and
pragmatic experience with faith. Within five years of the
writing of *The Heavenly City,* he was saying in *Progress
and Power* that even though today was dreary, tomorrow
might be better. Even though history could not justify
man's infinite perfectibility, the data did show that the
power of man's mind and hand had vastly increased. That
incredible tapping of new sources of power and relent-
lessly rapid utilization of new implements might out-
strip man's capacity to control the power he had released,
in which case mankind was embarked on a blind joy ride
that could end only in a cosmic smashup. Perhaps, al-
ternatively, the promise that new power held forth was
only that of progressive dehumanization of mankind,
only a steady advance toward the spiritual automation
of a humanity doomed to live the rhythmic group life of
happily conditioned termites and bees.

Leo Gershoy

He held it likely, when he wrote *Progress and Power,* that a far more cheerful solution impended. He thought it possible, with the rate of technological advance slowing up and the cultural lag narrowing, for man gradually to attain a high degree of social stability by "leaving it" to the machines. Leaving it to the machines meant, first, accepting life on the terms of a technological, industrialized civilization and, then, by social planning, adjusting his needs and many of his ways to it. The long-sought-for material security and social peace could then be attained, perhaps the scourges of war and poverty be abolished. In that happier tomorrow when man's power established the reality of progress, the sustaining idea would become irrelevant and unnecessary, and men could simply and modestly proclaim the worth of human values and their loyalty to them. With power ensuring material security, they would become free to enjoy as they could not now, in their time of troubles, the miracle of the mind—free to probe and test, learn and err, build and dream, and not cruelly be betrayed by their hopes.

In 1935, in *Progress and Power,* Becker was like Ulysses, happy in coming home from a long voyage. He was like Candide, after an eternity of disillusionment, finding solace in a final illusion—in the better world of tomorrow, better if not altogether new, in which man would at least have a chance to cultivate his garden with dignity, tolerance, and forebearance. Five years later still, in 1940, when the tide was running hard against the democracies, the reconciliation of stubborn facts and faith was completed. Becker's hesitation lay behind him. Fortunately, he wrote, some generalities still glittered, not least faith in humanity:

The Heavenly City *of Carl Becker*

To have faith in the dignity and worth of the individual man as an end in himself, to believe that it is better to be governed by persuasion than by coercion, . . . to believe that in the long run all values are inseparable from the love of truth and the disinterested search for it, to believe that knowledge and the power it confers should be used to promote the welfare and happiness of all men . . . —these are the values which are affirmed by the traditional democratic ideology. But they are older and more universal than democracy and do not depend upon it. They have a life of their own apart from any particular social system or type of civilization.[5]

Condorcet, hiding alas in vain to escape death, found solace for his fate in penning his triumphant *Sketch of the Progress of the Human Mind.* To Becker, with Nazism overrunning the bulwarks of democracy, also were given the consolations of philosophy. In *The Heavenly City* he had reached the conclusion that it was man's fate to seek the thread of justice in the labyrinthine processes of history. That conclusion he reaffirmed in his last years—not with the old ironic disclaimer that hope of salvation was an empty one, but with relief that there were consoling lessons still to be learned from the eternal flux. If faith in infinite progress was not one of them, happily there were other values to defeat despair and imbue men like himself with guarded hope for the future. The wave of the future was the wave of the eternal past, neither the determinism of Thomas nor of Condorcet, but man's freedom to stand or fall, man's responsibility to man for his moment on earth.

[5] "Some Generalities That Still Glitter," *Yale Review,* XXIX (June, 1940), 666.

Index*

* Except at the beginning of main headings, references to *The Heavenly City* and to Becker will be cited as *The H.C.* and B. throughout the index.

209

Index

Index

Index

Enlightenment, distortion of, 68

not shown as a breach in Western tradition, 57

literary quality, 52

scientific naturalism, confused with the modern mind, 56

social science, limited treatment of, 65

title, limitations imposed by, 60

Drouet, Juliette, 82

Edwards, Lyford P., 165

Einstein, A., 116

Empiricism, 18th-century, 34 (n.14), 37, 41, 64

Encyclopédie, 14, 21

Enlightenment:

B.'s challenge (?) of traditional concepts of, 68-69, 170, 189

B.'s effort to debunk, 49

breach in Western tradition, 63, 64, 68, 177-178

cause of the Revolution for B., xii, xv, 114, 164

Descartes' impact on, 15ff

distorted implications of *The H.C.,* 50, 68, 132, 144, 152f, 184

18th century as a secularization of Christianity, 126

faith, critique of B.'s comparison of 13th- and 18th-century approaches, 33, 144

natural law, and nature, approaches to, 17, 38-42, 59, 92, 147-148

Stoic roots, 17, 35-36, 40, 59, 148-149

new ideology for B., xiv

reason, critique of B.'s view in *The H.C.,* 32, 56ff, 91, 144ff

truth, its concept of, 183

see also *Philosophes, The H.C.*

Enragés, 111

Entstehung des Historismus, Die (Meinecke), 60

Epictetus, 36

Epicureanism, 50

Erkenntnis Problem (Cassirer), 11

"Everyman His Own Historian" (B.), xi, 75, 199

Evil, problem of:

central concern for B., 90ff

18th-century dilemma, B.'s version as false, 46

in Middle Ages and 18th century, 192

Marquis de Sade on, 47 (n.25)

Rousseau on, 46-47

Voltaire on, 47 (n.25)

Fontenelle, B., 20, 22, 117, 118

Fox, Edward H., xxiv

on B.:

anti-historian?, 184

Good (Truth) and Evil, approach to, 187

his students as his interpreters, 179

213

Index

epistemology, his solution, 202-205

historiography, views on, 199ff

humanism, triumph of in B., 205-206

and reason, his skepticism, 197-202

product of the disillusioned 1920s, 197

on *The H.C.:*

and the climate of the 1930s, 197-198

case of critics restated, 193-195

case study in B.'s historical relativism, 199

deliberately stresses similarities of preconceptions and thinking processes, 191-193

dissimilarities, B.'s awareness of, 190-191

heterodox thesis, 189

limited objective, 190

phase of B.'s reflection on liberalism, 198, 202

reflection of B.'s loss of faith in progress, 197

response to critics, 195-197

style, 193-194

thesis restated, B.'s argument, 190ff

Gibbon, E., 48, 147

Goethe, J. W. von, 25

Gottschalk, Louis, xii, xx, xxiii, 74, 115, 124, 135, 176

on *The H.C.:*

B. aware of dissimilarities, 90

evil, as a problem for all men to B., 95

as B.'s focus, 90-91

history as a substitute for Christian morality, the thesis, 93

limited purpose, 89-90

progress as substitute for immortality, the thesis, 94

reason and nature, the thesis, 92-93

style, doubts on, 89

thesis sound on rereading, 89

Greenlaw, Ralph, xxi

Grimm, J. L., 150

Grotius, H., 40

Guerlac, Henry, xx, xxii, xxiii, 86

on B.:

knowledge of science, 11

on reassessments, 4

personality, 3

teacher, 5

on 18th-century science:

breadth of concerns, 13

Cartesian influence, 15, 22ff

philosophes as serious scientists, 19

recent scholarship concerning, 9ff

on *The H.C.:*

and six erroneous notions re 18th-century science, 6-7

as a *jeu d'esprit*, 5

falsity of its empiricist interpretation of Galileo and Newton, 16

215

Index

Index

Index

thesis misconstrued by readers, 7, 67, 74-75, 90ff, 136, 142-143
thought, frozen by instead of provoked, 51
unwarranted, 28
—MS changes:
MSS available, 98
re Ancients and the Moderns, 117
re B.'s objectives, 102
re climate of opinion, 105
re Dante, 108
re 18th century's religious conceptions, 119
re idea of progress, 113
re the dedication, 101
re Voltaire, 109
revisions, types of, 99
—Purpose:
as a divergent view, 170
as a *jeu d'esprit,* 5, 28, 74-76, 87, 105, 135, 141
as a "trial run," 142, 166
as the book B. intended to write, 67
limited objective, 66, 190
reasons for writing, 132, 134, 162
—Reviewers, vii-x, 28 (n.3), 28 (n.5), 54, 143
—Style, 5, 27, 52, 67, 74, 89, 121, 123, 124, 132, 132-135, 141, 166, 172, 176, 189, 193
—Thesis and Argument:
and idea of progress, 117
continuity and change in

history, B. poses problem of, 30
ethics, how the *philosophes* dealt with it as the main concern, 91
similarity of 13th- and 18th-century approaches, 90
wherein B. rightly stresses continuity of Christian values, 59
heterodox thesis, 189
history and the *philosophe* search for morality, 93
natural law and the dilemma of evil, 92
philosophe debt to Aquinas, 92
progress as a substitute for immortality, 94
similarities stressed between Middle Ages and 18th century, 191
thesis, vii, 29, 58, 136
upheld, 89
—Title imposing exorbitant limits, 60, 62-63, 68, 135
Hegel, G., 41
Helvétius, C. A., 37
Histoire de Charles XII (Voltaire), 46
Historical Inevitability (Berlin), 65
Historical relativism, 77, 119, 129

219

Index

and the idea of progress,
117ff
Labrousse and B. on
causes of revolution,
114-115
little known in Europe, 98
MS changes, 99-120 *passim*
MSS of, 98-99

Ideas, role of, xiiff, 114ff, 130,
132, 164
Ideology, xxxi
*Intermédiaire des chercheurs
et curieux*, 79
Interpretation of Nature (Morgan), 57
Italian   Renaissance,   The
(Burckhardt), 68

James, William, xxxii, 198
Jameson, J. F., 194
Jansenism, 38, 145
Jeans, J. H., 153
Jefferson, Thomas, xxxi, 20, 58
Johnson, Samuel, 51

Kant, E., 76
Khrushchev, Nikita, 188
Kistler, Jonathan, xxii

Labrousse, Ernest, 114
La Mettrie, J. O. de, 111
Lanson, Gustave, 52
Lavoisier, A. L., 20, 23
Le Bon, Gustave, 165
Lectures, University of Virginia (B.), 137

Lenin, Nicolai, 131
Lerner, Max, vii
Lespinasse, Julie de, 150
Libby, Margaret, 9
Liberalism, B.'s reflections on,
202ff
"Liberalism—A Way Station,"
(B.), xi
Lincoln, Abraham, 200
Linnaeus, C., 13
Lipsius, Justus, 40
Littauer   Foundation,   Inc.,
Lucius N., xxv
Locke, John, xii, 33, 43, 59,
65, 178, 181
Lorwin, Val, 177
Louis XIV, 117

Machiavelli, 186
Maclaurin, C., 8
Maistre, Joseph de, 131
Mandelbaum, Maurice, 55
Marat, J. P., 24
Martin, Kingsley, 52, 195
Marx, Karl, xxxi, 125
Marxists, 95, 201
Materialism, 18th-century, 110
its Cartesian roots, 15, 24
impact of Neo-Stoicism, 24
Maupertuis, P. L. M. de, 21,
23
Meinecke, Friedrich, his analysis of 18th-century contributions   to   historical
writing, 60-62
Mencken, H. C., 154
Modern History (B.), xi, xiv,
75, 163
Modern   Predicament,   The
(Paton), 57

221

Index

Index

Index

Index

perception of Newton, 19
studies re his scientific knowledge, 9 (n.3)

Wade, Ira O., viii, 9, 28 (n.3)
Whewell, William, 11

Whitehead, Alfred N., 11, 105, 153, 190
influence on B., 31

Zerfall des Christlichen Ethos in XIX Jahrhundert (Steinbüchel), 57